Nutshell Series
Hornbook Series
and
Black Letter Series
of
WEST PUBLISHING
P.O. Box 64526
St. Paul, Minnesota 55164–0526

Accounting

FARIS' ACCOUNTING AND LAW IN A NUTSHELL, 377 pages, 1984. Softcover. (Text)

Administrative Law

AMAN AND MAYTON'S HORNBOOK ON ADMINISTRATIVE LAW, 917 pages, 1993. (Text)

GELLHORN AND LEVIN'S ADMINISTRATIVE LAW AND PROCESS IN A NUTSHELL, Third Edition, 479 pages, 1990. Softcover. (Text)

Admiralty

MARAIST'S ADMIRALTY IN A NUTSHELL, Second Edition, 379 pages, 1988. Softcover. (Text)

SCHOENBAUM'S HORNBOOK ON ADMIRALTY AND MARITIME LAW, Student Edition, 692 pages, 1987 with 1992 pocket part. (Text)

Agency—Partnership

REUSCHLEIN AND GREGORY'S HORNBOOK ON THE LAW OF AGENCY AND PARTNERSHIP, Second Edition, 683 pages, 1990. (Text)

STEFFEN'S AGENCY–PARTNERSHIP IN A NUTSHELL, 364 pages, 1977. Softcover. (Text)

Alternative Dispute Resolution

NOLAN–HALEY'S ALTERNATIVE DISPUTE RESOLUTION IN A NUTSHELL, 298 pages, 1992. Softcover. (Text)

RISKIN'S DISPUTE RESOLUTION FOR LAWYERS VIDEO TAPES, 1992. (Available for purchase by schools and libraries.)

American Indian Law

CANBY'S AMERICAN INDIAN LAW IN A NUTSHELL, Second Edition,

American Indian Law—Continued

336 pages, 1988. Softcover. (Text)

Antitrust—see also Regulated Industries, Trade Regulation

GELLHORN AND KOVACIC'S ANTITRUST LAW AND ECONOMICS IN A NUTSHELL, Fourth Edition, approximately 475 pages, 1993. Softcover. (Text)

HOVENKAMP'S BLACK LETTER ON ANTITRUST, Second Edition, 347 pages, 1993. Softcover. (Review)

HOVENKAMP'S HORNBOOK ON ECONOMICS AND FEDERAL ANTITRUST LAW, Student Edition, 414 pages, 1985. (Text)

SULLIVAN'S HORNBOOK OF THE LAW OF ANTITRUST, 886 pages, 1977. (Text)

Appellate Advocacy—see Trial and Appellate Advocacy

Art Law

DUBOFF'S ART LAW IN A NUTSHELL, Second Edition, 350 pages, 1993. Softcover. (Text)

Banking Law

LOVETT'S BANKING AND FINANCIAL INSTITUTIONS LAW IN A NUTSHELL, Third Edition, 470 pages, 1992. Softcover. (Text)

Civil Procedure—see also Federal Jurisdiction and Procedure

CLERMONT'S BLACK LETTER ON CIVIL PROCEDURE, Third Edition, 318 pages, 1993. Softcover. (Review)

FRIEDENTHAL, KANE AND MILLER'S HORNBOOK ON CIVIL PROCEDURE, Second Edition, approximately 1000 pages, 1993. (Text)

KANE'S CIVIL PROCEDURE IN A NUTSHELL, Third Edition, 303 pages, 1991. Softcover. (Text)

SIEGEL'S HORNBOOK ON NEW YORK PRACTICE, Second Edition, Student Edition, 1068 pages, 1991. Softcover. (Text) 1993–94 Supplement.

SLOMANSON AND WINGATE'S CALIFORNIA CIVIL PROCEDURE IN A NUTSHELL, 230 pages, 1992. Softcover. (Text)

Commercial Law

BAILEY AND HAGEDORN'S SECURED TRANSACTIONS IN A NUTSHELL, Third Edition, 390 pages, 1988. Softcover. (Text)

HENSON'S HORNBOOK ON SECURED TRANSACTIONS UNDER THE U.C.C., Second Edition, 504 pages, 1979, with 1979 pocket part. (Text)

MEYER AND SPEIDEL'S BLACK LETTER ON SALES AND LEASES OF GOODS, 317 pages, 1993. Softcover. (Review)

NICKLES' BLACK LETTER ON NEGOTIABLE INSTRUMENTS (AND OTHER RELATED COMMERCIAL PA-

Commercial Law—Continued

PER), Second Edition, 574 pages, 1993. Softcover. (Review)

SPEIDEL AND NICKLES' NEGOTIABLE INSTRUMENTS AND CHECK COLLECTION IN A NUTSHELL, Fourth Edition, 544 pages, 1993. Softcover. (Text)

STOCKTON AND MILLER'S SALES AND LEASES OF GOODS IN A NUTSHELL, Third Edition, 441 pages, 1992. Softcover. (Text)

STONE'S UNIFORM COMMERCIAL CODE IN A NUTSHELL, Third Edition, 580 pages, 1989. Softcover. (Text)

WHITE AND SUMMERS' HORNBOOK ON THE UNIFORM COMMERCIAL CODE, Third Edition, Student Edition, 1386 pages, 1988 with 1993 pocket part (covering Rev. Arts. 3, 4, new 2A, 4A). (Text)

Community Property

MENNELL AND BOYKOFF'S COMMUNITY PROPERTY IN A NUTSHELL, Second Edition, 432 pages, 1988. Softcover. (Text)

Comparative Law

GLENDON, GORDON AND OSAKWE'S COMPARATIVE LEGAL TRADITIONS IN A NUTSHELL. 402 pages, 1982. Softcover. (Text)

Conflict of Laws

HAY'S BLACK LETTER ON CONFLICT OF LAWS, 330 pages, 1989. Softcover. (Review)

SCOLES AND HAY'S HORNBOOK ON CONFLICT OF LAWS, Student Edition, 1160 pages, 1992. (Text)

SIEGEL'S CONFLICTS IN A NUTSHELL, 470 pages, 1982. Softcover. (Text)

Constitutional Law—Civil Rights

BARRON AND DIENES' BLACK LETTER ON CONSTITUTIONAL LAW, Third Edition, 440 pages, 1991. Softcover. (Review)

BARRON AND DIENES' CONSTITUTIONAL LAW IN A NUTSHELL, Second Edition, 483 pages, 1991. Softcover. (Text)

ENGDAHL'S CONSTITUTIONAL FEDERALISM IN A NUTSHELL, Second Edition, 411 pages, 1987. Softcover. (Text)

MARKS AND COOPER'S STATE CONSTITUTIONAL LAW IN A NUTSHELL, 329 pages, 1988. Softcover. (Text)

NOWAK AND ROTUNDA'S HORNBOOK ON CONSTITUTIONAL LAW, Fourth Edition, 1357 pages, 1991. (Text)

VIEIRA'S CONSTITUTIONAL CIVIL RIGHTS IN A NUTSHELL, Second Edition, 322 pages, 1990. Softcover. (Text)

WILLIAMS' CONSTITUTIONAL ANALYSIS IN A NUTSHELL, 388 pages, 1979. Softcover. (Text)

Consumer Law—see also Commercial Law.

EPSTEIN AND NICKLES' CONSUMER LAW IN A NUTSHELL, Second Edition, 418 pages, 1981. Softcover. (Text)

Contracts

CALAMARI AND PERILLO'S BLACK LETTER ON CONTRACTS, Second Edition, 462 pages, 1990. Softcover. (Review)

CALAMARI AND PERILLO'S HORNBOOK ON CONTRACTS, Third Edition, 1049 pages, 1987. (Text)

CORBIN'S TEXT ON CONTRACTS, One Volume Student Edition, 1224 pages, 1952. (Text)

FRIEDMAN'S CONTRACT REMEDIES IN A NUTSHELL, 323 pages, 1981. Softcover. (Text)

KEYES' GOVERNMENT CONTRACTS IN A NUTSHELL, Second Edition, 557 pages, 1990. Softcover. (Text)

SCHABER AND ROHWER'S CONTRACTS IN A NUTSHELL, Third Edition, 457 pages, 1990. Softcover. (Text)

Copyright—see Intellectual Property

Corporations

HAMILTON'S BLACK LETTER ON CORPORATIONS, Third Edition, 732 pages, 1992. Softcover. (Review)

HAMILTON'S THE LAW OF CORPO-RATIONS IN A NUTSHELL, Third Edition, 518 pages, 1991. Softcover. (Text)

HENN AND ALEXANDER'S HORNBOOK ON LAWS OF CORPORATIONS, Third Edition, Student Edition, 1371 pages, 1983, with 1986 pocket part. (Text)

Corrections

KRANTZ' THE LAW OF CORRECTIONS AND PRISONERS' RIGHTS IN A NUTSHELL, Third Edition, 407 pages, 1988. Softcover. (Text)

Creditors' Rights

EPSTEIN'S DEBTOR–CREDITOR LAW IN A NUTSHELL, Fourth Edition, 401 pages, 1991. Softcover. (Text)

EPSTEIN, NICKLES AND WHITE'S HORNBOOK ON BANKRUPTCY, 1077 pages, 1992. (Text)

NICKLES AND EPSTEIN'S BLACK LETTER ON CREDITORS' RIGHTS AND BANKRUPTCY, 576 pages, 1989. (Review)

Criminal Law and Criminal Procedure—see also Corrections, Juvenile Justice

ISRAEL AND LaFAVE'S CRIMINAL PROCEDURE—CONSTITUTIONAL LIMITATIONS IN A NUTSHELL, Fifth Edition, 475 pages, 1993. Softcover. (Text)

LaFAVE AND ISRAEL'S HORNBOOK ON CRIMINAL PROCEDURE, Second Edition, 1309 pages, 1992 with 1992 pocket part. (Text)

Criminal Law and Criminal Procedure—Continued

LAFAVE AND SCOTT'S HORNBOOK ON CRIMINAL LAW, Second Edition, 918 pages, 1986 with 1993 pocket part. (Text)

LOEWY'S CRIMINAL LAW IN A NUTSHELL, Second Edition, 321 pages, 1987. Softcover. (Text)

LOW'S BLACK LETTER ON CRIMINAL LAW, Revised First Edition, 443 pages, 1990. Softcover. (Review)

PODGOR'S WHITE COLLAR CRIME IN A NUTSHELL, Approximately 300 pages, 1993. Softcover. (Text)

SUBIN, MIRSKY AND WEINSTEIN'S THE CRIMINAL PROCESS: PROSECUTION AND DEFENSE FUNCTIONS, 470 pages, 1993. Softcover. Teacher's Manual available. (Text)

Domestic Relations

CLARK'S HORNBOOK ON DOMESTIC RELATIONS, Second Edition, Student Edition, 1050 pages, 1988. (Text)

KRAUSE'S BLACK LETTER ON FAMILY LAW, 314 pages, 1988. Softcover. (Review)

KRAUSE'S FAMILY LAW IN A NUTSHELL, Second Edition, 444 pages, 1986. Softcover. (Text)

MALLOY'S LAW AND ECONOMICS: A COMPARATIVE APPROACH TO THEORY AND PRACTICE, 166 pages, 1990. Softcover. (Text)

Education Law

ALEXANDER AND ALEXANDER'S THE LAW OF SCHOOLS, STUDENTS AND TEACHERS IN A NUTSHELL, 409 pages, 1984. Softcover. (Text)

Employment Discrimination—see also Gender Discrimination

PLAYER'S FEDERAL LAW OF EMPLOYMENT DISCRIMINATION IN A NUTSHELL, Third Edition, 338 pages, 1992. Softcover. (Text)

PLAYER'S HORNBOOK ON EMPLOYMENT DISCRIMINATION LAW, Student Edition, 708 pages, 1988. (Text)

Energy and Natural Resources Law—see also Oil and Gas

LAITOS AND TOMAIN'S ENERGY AND NATURAL RESOURCES LAW IN A NUTSHELL, 554 pages, 1992. Softcover. (Text)

Environmental Law—see also Energy and Natural Resources Law; Sea, Law of

CAMPBELL–MOHN, BREEN AND FUTRELL'S ENVIRONMENTAL LAW: FROM RESOURCES TO RECOVERY, (Environmental Law Institute) Approximately 975 pages, 1993. (Text)

FINDLEY AND FARBER'S ENVIRONMENTAL LAW IN A NUTSHELL, Third Edition, 355 pages, 1992.

Environmental Law—Continued Softcover. (Text)

RODGERS' HORNBOOK ON ENVIRONMENTAL LAW, 956 pages, 1977, with 1984 pocket part. (Text)

Equity—see Remedies

Estate Planning—see also Trusts and Estates; Taxation—Estate and Gift

LYNN'S INTRODUCTION TO ESTATE PLANNING IN A NUTSHELL, Fourth Edition, 352 pages, 1992. Softcover. (Text)

Evidence

BROUN AND BLAKEY'S BLACK LETTER ON EVIDENCE, 269 pages, 1984. Softcover. (Review)

GRAHAM'S FEDERAL RULES OF EVIDENCE IN A NUTSHELL, Third Edition, 486 pages, 1992. Softcover. (Text)

LILLY'S AN INTRODUCTION TO THE LAW OF EVIDENCE, Second Edition, 585 pages, 1987. (Text)

MCCORMICK'S HORNBOOK ON EVIDENCE, Fourth Edition, Student Edition, 672 pages, 1992. (Text)

ROTHSTEIN'S EVIDENCE IN A NUTSHELL: STATE AND FEDERAL RULES, Second Edition, 514 pages, 1981. Softcover. (Text)

Federal Jurisdiction and Procedure

CURRIE'S FEDERAL JURISDICTION IN A NUTSHELL, Third Edition, 242 pages, 1990. Softcover. (Text)

REDISH'S BLACK LETTER ON FEDERAL JURISDICTION, Second Edition, 234 pages, 1991. Softcover. (Review)

WRIGHT'S HORNBOOK ON FEDERAL COURTS, Fourth Edition, Student Edition, 870 pages, 1983. (Text)

First Amendment

BARRON AND DIENES' FIRST AMENDMENT LAW IN A NUTSHELL, Approximately 450 pages, September, 1993 pub. Softcover. (Text)

GARVEY AND SCHAUER'S THE FIRST AMENDMENT: A READER, 527 pages, 1992. Softcover. (Reader)

Future Interests—see Trusts and Estates

Gender Discrimination—see also Employment Discrimination

THOMAS' SEX DISCRIMINATION IN A NUTSHELL, Second Edition, 395 pages, 1991. Softcover. (Text)

Health Law—see Medicine, Law and

Human Rights—see International Law

Immigration Law

WEISSBRODT'S IMMIGRATION LAW AND PROCEDURE IN A NUTSHELL,

Immigration Law—Continued
Third Edition, 497 pages, 1992. Softcover. (Text)

Indian Law—see American Indian Law

Insurance Law

DOBBYN'S INSURANCE LAW IN A NUTSHELL, Second Edition, 316 pages, 1989. Softcover. (Text)

KEETON AND WIDISS' INSURANCE LAW, Student Edition, 1359 pages, 1988. (Text)

Intellectual Property Law—see also Trade Regulation

MILLER AND DAVIS' INTELLECTUAL PROPERTY—PATENTS, TRADEMARKS AND COPYRIGHT IN A NUTSHELL, Second Edition, 437 pages, 1990. Softcover. (Text)

International Law—see also Sea, Law of

BUERGENTHAL'S INTERNATIONAL HUMAN RIGHTS IN A NUTSHELL, 283 pages, 1988. Softcover. (Text)

BUERGENTHAL AND MAIER'S PUBLIC INTERNATIONAL LAW IN A NUTSHELL, Second Edition, 275 pages, 1990. Softcover. (Text)

FOLSOM'S EUROPEAN COMMUNITY LAW IN A NUTSHELL, 423 pages, 1992. Softcover. (Text)

FOLSOM, GORDON AND SPANOGLE'S INTERNATIONAL BUSINESS TRANSACTIONS IN A NUTSHELL, Fourth Edition, 548

pages, 1992. Softcover. (Text)

Interviewing and Counseling

SHAFFER AND ELKINS' LEGAL INTERVIEWING AND COUNSELING IN A NUTSHELL, Second Edition, 487 pages, 1987. Softcover. (Text)

Introduction to Law—see Legal Method and Legal System

Introduction to Law Study

HEGLAND'S INTRODUCTION TO THE STUDY AND PRACTICE OF LAW IN A NUTSHELL, 418 pages, 1983. Softcover. (Text)

KINYON'S INTRODUCTION TO LAW STUDY AND LAW EXAMINATIONS IN A NUTSHELL, 389 pages, 1971. Softcover. (Text)

Judicial Process—see Legal Method and Legal System

SINHA'S JURISPRUDENCE (LEGAL PHILOSOPHY) IN A NUTSHELL. 379 pages, 1993. Softcover. (Text)

Juvenile Justice

FOX'S JUVENILE COURTS IN A NUTSHELL, Third Edition, 291 pages, 1984. Softcover. (Text)

Labor and Employment Law—see also Employment Discrimination, Workers' Compensation

CONISON'S EMPLOYEE BENEFIT PLANS IN A NUTSHELL, Approximately 465 pages, 1993. Softcover. (Text)

Labor and Employment Law— Continued

LESLIE'S LABOR LAW IN A NUT-SHELL, Third Edition, 388 pages, 1992. Softcover. (Text)

NOLAN'S LABOR ARBITRATION LAW AND PRACTICE IN A NUT-SHELL, 358 pages, 1979. Soft-cover. (Text)

Land Finance—Property Securi-ty—see Real Estate Transactions

Land Use

HAGMAN AND JUERGENSMEYER'S HORNBOOK ON URBAN PLANNING AND LAND DEVELOPMENT CON-TROL LAW, Second Edition, Student Edition, 680 pages, 1986. (Text)

WRIGHT AND WRIGHT'S LAND USE IN A NUTSHELL, Second Edition, 356 pages, 1985. Softcover. (Text)

Legal History—see also Legal Method and Legal System

Legal Method and Legal Sys-tem—see also Legal Re-search, Legal Writing

KEMPIN'S HISTORICAL INTRODUC-TION TO ANGLO-AMERICAN LAW IN A NUTSHELL, Third Edition, 323 pages, 1990. Softcover. (Text)

REYNOLDS' JUDICIAL PROCESS IN A NUTSHELL, Second Edition, 308 pages, 1991. Softcover. (Text)

Legal Research

COHEN AND OLSON'S LEGAL RE-SEARCH IN A NUTSHELL, Fifth Edition, 370 pages, 1992. Soft-cover. (Text)

COHEN, BERRING AND OLSON'S HORNBOOK ON HOW TO FIND THE LAW, Ninth Edition, 716 pages, 1989. (Text)

HAZELTON'S COMPUTER–ASSISTED LEGAL RESEARCH: THE BASICS, Approximately 70 pages, 1993. Softcover. (Coursebook)

Legal Writing and Drafting

MELLINKOFF'S DICTIONARY OF AMERICAN LEGAL USAGE, 703 pages, 1992. Softcover. (Text)

SQUIRES AND ROMBAUER'S LEGAL WRITING IN A NUTSHELL, 294 pages, 1982. Softcover. (Text)

Legislation—see also Legal Writing and Drafting

DAVIES' LEGISLATIVE LAW AND PROCESS IN A NUTSHELL, Second Edition, 346 pages, 1986. Soft-cover. (Text)

Local Government

MCCARTHY'S LOCAL GOVERN-MENT LAW IN A NUTSHELL, Third Edition, 435 pages, 1990. Soft-cover. (Text)

REYNOLDS' HORNBOOK ON LOCAL GOVERNMENT LAW, 860 pages, 1982 with 1993 pocket part. (Text)

Securities Regulation—Continued

OF SECURITIES REGULATION, Second Edition, Student Edition, 1082 pages, 1990. (Text)

RATNER'S SECURITIES REGULATION IN A NUTSHELL, Fourth Edition, 320 pages, 1992. Softcover. (Text)

Sports Law

CHAMPION'S SPORTS LAW IN A NUTSHELL. 325 pages, 1993. Softcover. (Text)

SCHUBERT, SMITH AND TRENTADUE'S SPORTS LAW, 395 pages, 1986. (Text)

Tax Policy

DODGE'S THE LOGIC OF TAX, 343 pages, 1989. Softcover. (Text)

UTZ' TAX POLICY: AN INTRODUCTION AND SURVEY OF THE PRINCIPAL DEBATES, 260 pages, 1993. Softcover. Teacher's Manual available. (Coursebook)

Tax Practice and Procedure

MORGAN'S TAX PROCEDURE AND TAX FRAUD IN A NUTSHELL, 400 pages, 1990. Softcover. (Text)

Taxation—Corporate

SCHWARZ AND LATHROPE'S BLACK LETTER ON CORPORATE AND PARTNERSHIP TAXATION, 537 pages, 1991. Softcover. (Review)

WEIDENBRUCH AND BURKE'S FEDERAL INCOME TAXATION OF CORPORATIONS AND STOCKHOLDERS IN A NUTSHELL, Third Edition, 309 pages, 1989. Softcover. (Text)

Taxation—Estate & Gift—see also Estate Planning, Trusts and Estates

MCNULTY'S FEDERAL ESTATE AND GIFT TAXATION IN A NUTSHELL, Fourth Edition, 496 pages, 1989. Softcover. (Text)

PEAT AND WILLBANKS' FEDERAL ESTATE AND GIFT TAXATION: AN ANALYSIS AND CRITIQUE, 265 pages, 1991. Softcover. (Text)

Taxation—Individual

HUDSON AND LIND'S BLACK LETTER ON FEDERAL INCOME TAXATION, Fourth Edition, 410 pages, 1992. Softcover. (Review)

MCNULTY'S FEDERAL INCOME TAXATION OF INDIVIDUALS IN A NUTSHELL, Fourth Edition, 503 pages, 1988. Softcover. (Text)

POSIN'S FEDERAL INCOME TAXATION, Second Edition, approximately 550 pages, 1993. Softcover. (Text)

ROSE AND CHOMMIE'S HORNBOOK ON FEDERAL INCOME TAXATION, Third Edition, 923 pages, 1988, with 1991 pocket part. (Text)

Taxation—International

DOERNBERG'S INTERNATIONAL TAXATION IN A NUTSHELL, Second Edition, approximately 375 pages, 1993. Softcover. (Text)

BISHOP AND BROOKS' FEDERAL

Taxation—International—Continued

PARTNERSHIP TAXATION: A GUIDE TO THE LEADING CASES, STATUTES, AND REGULATIONS, 545 pages, 1990. Softcover. (Text)

BURKE'S FEDERAL INCOME TAXATION OF PARTNERSHIPS IN A NUTSHELL, 356 pages, 1992. Softcover. (Text)

SCHWARZ AND LATHROPE'S BLACK LETTER ON CORPORATE AND PARTNERSHIP TAXATION, 537 pages, 1991. Softcover. (Review)

Taxation—State & Local

GELFAND AND SALSICH'S STATE AND LOCAL TAXATION AND FINANCE IN A NUTSHELL, 309 pages, 1986. Softcover. (Text)

Torts—see also Products Liability

KIONKA'S BLACK LETTER ON TORTS, Second Edition, approximately 350 pages, 1993. Softcover. (Review)

KIONKA'S TORTS IN A NUTSHELL, Second Edition, 449 pages, 1992. Softcover. (Text)

PROSSER AND KEETON'S HORNBOOK ON TORTS, Fifth Edition, Student Edition, 1286 pages, 1984 with 1988 pocket part. (Text)

Trade Regulation—see also Antitrust, Regulated Industries

MCMANIS' UNFAIR TRADE PRACTICES IN A NUTSHELL, Third Edition, 471 pages, 1993. Softcover. (Text)

SCHECHTER'S BLACK LETTER ON UNFAIR TRADE PRACTICES AND INTELLECTUAL PROPERTY, Second Edition, approximately 300 pages, 1993. Softcover. (Review)

Trial and Appellate Advocacy—see also Civil Procedure

BERGMAN'S TRIAL ADVOCACY IN A NUTSHELL, Second Edition, 354 pages, 1989. Softcover. (Text)

CLARY'S PRIMER ON THE ANALYSIS AND PRESENTATION OF LEGAL ARGUMENT, 106 pages, 1992. Softcover. (Text)

DESSEM'S PRETRIAL LITIGATION IN A NUTSHELL, 382 pages, 1992. Softcover. (Text)

GOLDBERG'S THE FIRST TRIAL (WHERE DO I SIT? WHAT DO I SAY?) IN A NUTSHELL, 396 pages, 1982. Softcover. (Text)

HEGLAND'S TRIAL AND PRACTICE SKILLS IN A NUTSHELL, 346 pages, 1978. Softcover. (Text)

HORNSTEIN'S APPELLATE ADVOCACY IN A NUTSHELL, 325 pages, 1984. Softcover. (Text)

JEANS' TRIAL ADVOCACY, Second Edition, approximately 575

Advisory Board

[XIV]

APPELLATE ADVOCACY

IN A NUTSHELL

By

ALAN D. HORNSTEIN

Professor of Law
University of Maryland School of Law

ST. PAUL, MINN.
WEST PUBLISHING CO.
1984

COPYRIGHT © 1984 By WEST PUBLISHING CO.
                            610 Opperman Drive
                            P.O. Box 64526
                            St. Paul, MN 55164–0526

Library of Congress Cataloging in Publication Data

Hornstein, Alan D., 1945–
     Appellate advocacy in a nutshell.

     (Nutshell series)
     Includes index.
     1. Appellate procedure—United States. 2. Trial prac-
tice—United States. I. Title. II. Series.
KF9050.Z9H668   1984   347.73'8   84–5150
                              347.3078

ISBN 0–314–81456–6

Hornstein App.Advocacy N.S.
3rd Reprint—1994

For Brenda
Let me count the ways.

*

FOREWORD

The need for an appellate process arises from the innate realization of mankind that the human intellect and human justice are frail at their best. It is necessary therefore to measure one man's mind against another in order to purge the final result, so far as may be, of all passion, prejudice or infirmity. It is the effort to realize the maximum of justice in human relations; and to keep firm and stable the foundations on which all ordered society rests. There is no field of nobler usefulness for the lawyer. For him, who in the splendid words of Chancellor D'Aguesseau, belongs to an order "as old as the magistracy, as noble as virtue, as necessary as justice."

JOHN W. DAVIS
Address delivered before The Association of the Bar of the City of New York, October 22, 1940

*

PREFACE

This book grew out of my experience as coach and advisor to Maryland's National Moot Court Teams over a number of years—a responsibility I undertook with some reluctance and gave up with even greater reluctance. I learned as much from the men and women who made up those teams as they learned from me. Much of what I learned from observing the superb way in which they performed their roles as advocates is reflected in the pages that folllow. Their understanding that professional responsibility means more than not comingling clients' funds—that to be professionally responsible entails as well a dedication to one's craft—must surely be the hope of our often beleaguered profession. It is this insistence on maintaining the integrity of the argument that marks the advocate as a professional.

Others have also contributed generously to my understanding of the craft of advocacy. They are far too numerous to mention. A few, however, deserve special gratitude. The late Frederick vanPelt Bryan showed me what it means to be a judge, and hence what is required to persuade one. It was a privilege to know him and to see him in action. I am most appreciative of the support provided by the University of Maryland School of Law throughout the project. Bill Reynolds, Mike Millemann and Greg Young, all valued colleagues at Maryland, took time from their busy schedules to read sections of the manuscript. Mary Akerley, a member of the last team that I coached at Maryland served ably as my research and editorial assistant throughout the production of the book. She was always able to help make it a bit clearer, a bit more precise, a bit more accurate. It would have been far more difficult and less well executed without her unstinting assistance. The usual disclaimers, of course, apply.

Thanks must also go to the Faculty Secretaries at Maryland, but especially to Marilyn O'Neill whose ability to translate my chicken scratches into readable copy with speed and accuracy is surpassed only by the great good humor with which she manages it.

Finally, and most important, is my gratitude to the person to whom this book is dedicated: to my friend, lover, partner, wife. Thanks. Enough said.

ADH

February, 1984

OUTLINE

OUTLINE

*

APPELLATE ADVOCACY

IN A NUTSHELL

*

CHAPTER ONE

INTRODUCTION

This is a book about rhetoric. It is a subject that has lately come into disrepute. That is, perhaps, surprising when one considers that rhetoric was among the seven liberal arts of the medieval university; that, along with grammar and logic, and mediating between them, it formed the trivium of the arts of discourse. Yet it is often confused with propaganda, with clever attempts to persuade through pettifoggery, half truth or outright deception. That is a mistaken view of the art of rhetoric. More, for the appellate advocate, it is a disastrous view.

Rhetoric is the art of persuasion; but not every mode of persuasion is the exercise of that art. To persuade by half truth may sometimes be effective in the short run. It is, however, to rhetoric as plagiarism is to the art of writing. The kind of persuasion properly denominated rhetoric is that which is based upon a clear presentation of a position with the reasons supporting it thoroughly explicated, with its weaknesses revealed but shown to be outweighed by its strengths.

The concern in this *Nutshell* is with a particular kind of rhetoric: legal argument, more narrowly, argument presented to an appellate court with the purpose of obtaining a favorable decision. For the appellate advocate the exercise of rhetorical skill is as much a part of her craft as knowledge and understanding of the law. For without the ability to put her knowledge and understanding to effective use, they are no more than lovely paintings in a lightless room. Thus, to serve one's client, an understanding of the principles of effective appellate advocacy is essential. That is not, however, the only reason to master these skills.

All lawyers, all law students are familiar with appellate opinions. They express the common law, impart meaning to legislation, inform the counseling and advisory functions of the lawyer. They remain the principal source of instruction in American law schools. Surely the ultimate responsibility for the value (or lack of value) of an appellate opinion must be charged to the judge who writes it. Yet it is unrealistic to expect of judges as busy as we keep ours that their opinions be substantially better than the material provided them by the advocates whose responsibility it is to present the case, illuminate the issues to be decided and explicate the concerns that should inform those decisions. For good or ill, the opinion may be no more than the child of the two advocates that gave it life, with the judge serving simply as midwife. The appellate advocate, therefore, owes a duty not merely to her client but to the growth and development of the law. It is through her argument—oral and written—that the appellate advocate contributes to this growth and development. The better, the more professional and craftsmanlike that argument, the greater the contribution.

Consequently, to fail to maintain the highest standards of advocacy is not merely to disserve one's client, important as that is, it is also to default on one's responsibility as a professional. The resort to mere cleverness, to obfuscation, to half truth is to impeach the integrity of one's argument—upon which one's integrity as an advocate, as a professional, depends.

It is with the clear, informative but persuasive presentation of one's case to an appellate court that this *Nutshell* is concerned. Although, of course, a thorough knowledge of the substantive law relevant to one's case is essential to effective advocacy, our subject matter is not substantive law. The few citations to be found throughout the book are to illustrate particular kinds of arguments, techniques or concerns, and are not to explain or analyze any particular doctrinal position. Even there an attempt has been made to use cases or examples likely to be familiar to most readers.

Similarly, a persuasive argument must be grounded on thorough research of all relevant materials; yet the reader will search here in vain for advice on how to do legal research. That topic is entitled to a volume of its own and there are several excellent ones readily available.

As important as knowledge of the law and thorough research is the ability to write well—succinctly, cogently and clearly, if not elegantly—and to speak well, if one hopes to persuade. Those skills, too, are not addressed in this *Nutshell*, except incidentally. There are a number of books available that can assist one in improving her writing, fewer with respect to speaking ability.

Given knowledge of the required substantive law and the skills of research, writing and speaking, the aim of this *Nutshell* is to offer advice on what to do with that knowledge and those skills —how to use them to develop a presentation that is craftsmanlike, clear and persuasive.

The advice offered may sometimes appear to be in the form of a strange amalgamation of principles derived from the disciplines of legal process and jurisprudence, combined with nuts and bolts exploration of the strategy and tactics of appellate advocacy. Yet, it is that combination, both components of which are necessary to effective advocacy, that makes the craft so fascinating an object of study. It is only through an exploration of the nature and purpose of the various fields of law and of appellate courts at all levels that one can put to use one's strategic and tactical knowledge. A good general knows the terrain.

No mere book can accomplish more than to offer advice. As is true of the skills of other crafts, development of the skills of oral and written persuasion—of rhetoric—requires practice and observation and emulation of one's betters. Perhaps the best way to develop the skills of appellate advocacy is to read the briefs of good appellate lawyers and to attend their oral arguments. Even the observation of poor performances can be helpful. After reading a particular brief or observing an oral argument the reader should analyze what there was about the performance that was persuasive, what there was about it that did not work well. An excellent source of raw material for such an exercise is the series of volumes, *Landmark Briefs and Arguments of the Supreme Court of the United States*. These volumes contain the briefs in facsimile and transcripts of oral arguments in selected cases decided by the Supreme Court. Some are excellent, some not so good, but all are informative. The general availability of that material explains the absence of model briefs, typical of appellate advocacy books, within these covers. A study of that material, especially when read in conjunction with the opinions ultimately filed in those cases is a superb way of developing a sense of what appellate advocacy is all about.

CHAPTER TWO

EFFECTIVE ADVOCACY

§ 2–1. In General

The most important advice that can be given to an advocate is to remind her that she is an *advocate*. This apparently silly redundancy is often enough ignored, however, as to astonish those who have not themselves witnessed the lawyer who writes a brief as if it were a treatise or law review article and who presents an oral argument as if delivering a lecture to a group of students or, only slightly better, a bar association meeting.

It cannot be said too frequently that the job of the advocate is to persuade—to move the mind of the court to a conviction that the advocate's position should be upheld over that of her adversary. The great engine of that movement is the communication between the advocate and the court; thus, Daniel Webster's famous aphorism: "The power of clear statement is the great power at the bar." If the court cannot follow or understand what the advocate is saying it cannot be persuaded by her. Thus, at least in this sense,

[*6*]

one aspect of the advocate's role is to make the task of the court easier to perform. Fortunately, a persuasive presentation acomplishes this goal. More than hard cases, it is poor lawyers that make bad law.

There is another reason that the skills of advocacy are so important—important not only to fulfill the obligation owed to one's client, but to the development of the law itself. There was a time when an advocate took as much time as he required to present his case. The oral arguments in *McCulloch* v. *Maryland*, 17 U.S. (4 Wheat.) 316 (1819), for example, consumed some six days; and that was hardly unique. Similarly, the length of an advocate's written argument was dictated by what had to be said. Consequently, the necessity of sharpening one's argument, of distilling out of the mass of factual and legal detail the germ of the case, and focusing the court's attention on it was not as great. Eventually one would get to the point; there was no hurry. The court had time to listen and reflect, and the advocate could illuminate each dark nook and corner of the case.

Whether for good or ill, those times are long since past. The volume of litigation in our appellate courts has resulted in judges having less time to reflect on the nuances of each issue in each case, while advocates are given less time to perform their function of enlightening the court. The time allotted for oral argument has been shortened from days to minutes; briefs, too, are almost always required to adhere to prescribed page limitations.

The significance of this, of course, is that each moment, each word is all the more important. Arguments must be framed concisely and in such a way as to permit the court to grasp precisely what must be decided and what position the advocate has taken with respect to those issues. The nuances and subtleties of one's case, the richness of detail—all this must be thoroughly integrated into one's argument. Bits and pieces must not be permitted to lie about, so to speak, and dealt with as "by the way." The court simply lacks the time and patience to do the winnowing and pruning necessary to the aesthetic growth of the law. It is the job of the advocate to assist the court.

The art of effective communication—communication designed to move the mind of another to a particular belief—requires the mastery of certain techniques and rules. An appropriate metaphor might be that of the painter. Genius is helpful but not necessary. Craft, on the other hand, is essential. As with painting there are two levels at which the techniques that make up the craft must be appreciated. One is the molecular level,

the devices necessary to achieve particular effects
—use of shading, the way the brush is to be held,
the way movement or light is suggested. There
are also, however, molar principles—skills necessary to the production of any quality work within
a particular genre. In painting these principles
concern such things as perspective and composition. As applied to the art of appellate advocacy
they are thematic and structural in nature. The
finer techniques—those governing particular
kinds of arguments or particular bits and pieces
of arguments—are the subject matter of other
chapters. Here, we are concerned with the more
general thematic and structural issues which
must be considered in the formation and execution of any first rate bit of advocacy.

§ 2–2. The Theme

Perhaps the most important and helpful rhetorical device for effective appellate advocacy is the
argument's theme. The selection and development of this theme may be the most difficult and
most important decision made by the advocate.
The purpose of the theme is to serve as an organizing and integrating principle around which the
argument will be built. The theme will dictate
the argument in much the same way that the
skeleton dictates the shape of an animal.

A useful theme must, first, be as simple and as
simply stated as the case permits. Ideally, it

should state a principle which the reader or listener can grasp as a unitary concept requiring as little cognitive mediation as possible. Second, it ought to serve as foundation, conclusion, and summary of everything else the advocate has to communicate. A well constructed theme suggests not only the desired result but the reasoning upon which that result is based. It crystallizes the issue in a way that suggests its appropriate resolution and the justification for that resolution. The ability to reduce a complicated case to one or two starkly simple notions is of great importance to the knowledgeable advocate. It provides an advantage worthy of cultivation. Finally, a good theme reflects the legal principle at the heart of the argument as well as the policy upon which that principle is based. Moreover, the policy justification ought to be framed in common sense terms that appeal immediately to the understanding of even the most primitive legal intellect.

Obviously, there is a lot of baggage to be borne by the theme of one's argument. Just as obviously, carrying that baggage to its destination requires thorough analysis of the relevant law and the facts as developed in the procedural context dictated by the record. It is only in that way that the advocate can formulate and develop the theme of her case. To the extent that this is not done—or not done well—the entire case will be perceived as that much weaker.

Not only is the theme important to the persuasive force of the argument because of its direct effect on the audience, it also provides substantial collateral advantages to the advocate. Once the theme has been developed (it will continue to be refined throughout the entire appellate advocacy process), it assists in virtually every other facet of preparation and execution of the work to be done on the case, from determining how to structure the argument and use the cases and other authorities to responding to questions at oral argument while retaining the ability to return to the focus of one's oral presentation.

In short, a good theme enables the advocate to maintain control of her argument.

It may be helpful to provide an example of the theme of an argument. Among the more fashionable issues in recent cases has been the extent to which it is permissible to deny a demand for a jury trial on the grounds that the case is too complex—either factually or legally—for a lay jury to comprehend. If one were preparing the appeal of the case in which a demand for a jury trial had been struck on these grounds, what might be a good theme for each side to use as the basis of its presentation?

It should be obvious that the final decision on this question must await a substantial amount of legal research, for the theme must reflect the doctrinal basis of the argument. Nonetheless, most advocates probably know enough already to be able to generate at least a working theme, subject, of course, to substantial refinement as the work progresses. Research will reveal that there is a seventh amendment right to a jury in federal courts in cases at common law. Thus, appellee must either find some constitutional basis for excepting the case from the seventh amendment command or must show that it was never intended to be included within that amendment. A possible theme for the advocate seeking a bench trial might be: "Litigants' rights ought not to be at the mercy of the caprice of an incompetent jury."

There are a number of noteworthy features about this statement. First, the use of the word "caprice" in conjunction with the word "rights" calls to the lawyer's mind the notion of arbitrary and capricious denial of rights. The use of the word "incompetent" to modify the word "jury" suggests two things: first, that the advocate is not seeking any sort of blanket denial of the right to jury trial, but only an unwillingness to submit to certain instances of jury determination. Thus there is an inherent limiting principle to the advocate's position. Second, there is an instantaneous common sense appeal to the notion that one ought not to commit important decisions to those not competent to make them. Finally, the phrase, "at the mercy of" suggests unprincipled decisionmaking.

Much of the legal research to be done in the case will support and tie into this theme. As just one example, it will be discovered that the right extends to common law cases but not to equity cases. One might use this to make the point that equitable accounting, although it results in a money judgment, is not triable to a jury perhaps because of the inherent complexity of the accounting procedure. Notice that this supports the denial of a jury trial in a suit for money damages, a traditional common law remedy.

The party seeking the jury trial, on the other hand, might suggest as her theme something like the jury as representatives of the common sense and values of the community. She, of course, then would try to characterize the facts of the case and the issues presented as being well within the traditional province of the jury. For example, to the extent that different witnesses offer conflicting testimony on some relatively complex and intricate question of fact, the advocate favoring the jury determination would characterize the question as being largely one of credibility.

What is important to see here is that each side can crystallize its argument in a very few words —"the caprice of an incompetent jury," "the common sense of the community"—easily grasped by a busy court. Moreover, the arguments on both sides can be formed to support and expand upon these quite simply stated notions. To the extent that they do so, the arguments will have an integrity that will make them not only more easily comprehended but more persuasive as well.

§ 2–3. The Structure

Once a theme has been formulated the advocate must organize the issues to be argued and the points to be made in a way that is at once analytically appropriate and supportive of the theme. In doing so it is important to keep in mind the role of the appellate court (discussed in greater detail in Chapter Three) as the reviewer of rulings made by an inferior court.

Unfortunately, among the major differences between real world appellate practice and the academic moot court programs and competitions that purport to be its training ground is the importance in the former and the virtual nonexistence in the latter of issue selection. The practitioner's skill in selecting from among the various actions of the inferior court those most open to attack is critically important to success on the appellate level. Yet the law school typically omits this phase of appellate practice altogether. Generally problems are presented in the form of either the lower court opinion giving rise to the appeal, or, still worse, a canned statement of the controversy prepared by the inventors of the problem. It is rare that students have the opportunity to develop the skill of discerning from the hundreds or thousands of pages of a trial record the relatively few portions that may support a successful appeal.

After the rulings upon which the appeal is to rest have been selected they must be coaxed and massaged until they have been transformed into issues, phrased more or less abstractly, that will appeal to the superior court. These issues must then be organized in a way that is most supportive of the advocate's position and most helpful to the understanding of the court.

It is generally not helpful to an appellant to include excessive assignments of error or an excessive number of issues to present to the appellate court. Rather than impressing the court, an interminable number of issues is likely to dilute the effect of even those that may be worthy. As with any art, the key lies in judicious exclusion of what is not helpful or necessary. If it is necessary—and the case where it is will be rare—to include a great number of assignments of error or of issues they should at least be grouped under a small number of more general topics, lest the list appear unmanageable.

Judge Godbold of the United States Court of Appeals for the Fifth Circuit has described precisely what not to do:

> . . . I have in my files the briefs in a civil case in which there are either five or six issues depending upon how one wishes to slice them. The appellant's brief states them as twenty-two issues. The appellee restates and regroups them into sixteen issues. The reply brief disagrees with appellee's restatement and contains a partial third regrouping. In appellee's brief each restated point begins with a statement about like this: "This point covers appellant's points 2, 5, and first half of 7, and the second half of 14." To make our way through this maze my clerk and I prepared a mammoth chart with lines, arrows, and boxes, making the necessary consolidation and separations and rationally redefining the issues. It looks like the organizational chart for the Department of Health, Education and Welfare. In the box where each issue is described is a notation like this: "Read pp. 4–6, 14–17 and 42–44, Brief I; pp. 19–22 and 31–35 of Brief II; pp. 2–3 and 10 of Brief III."

J. Godbold, *Twenty Pages and Twenty Minutes— Effective Advocacy on Appeal*, 30 Sw.L.J. 801, 810 (1976).

The Questions Presented in the briefs filed in *Heffron* v. *International Society for Krishna Consciousness*, 452 U.S. 640, 101 S.Ct. 2559 (1981), are also instructive.   The petitioners, managers of the Minnesota State Fair, presented only one question for decision:

> May the International Society for Krishna Consciousness and its members be exempt, under the First Amendment, from a Minnesota State Fair rule which requires that all persons or organizations who solicit money or sell or distribute materials during the annual 12-day fair do so only from a fixed location on the fairgrounds, when that rule is applied equally to all persons without regard to the content of their materials or religious beliefs?

By contrast, the respondent listed six, only the last of which is reproduced here as typical of the set:

> Would sustaining the invalidation of the booth rule as to non-commercial distribution and solicitation leave the state helpless to cope with confusion and congestion at its annual fair?

[The curious reader is referred to 126 *Landmark Briefs and Arguments of the Supreme Court of the United States: Constitutional Law, 1980 Term Supplement* 113 (1981), for the others.

There probably could be no better learning exercise than to read the briefs and oral arguments in *Heffron*, and then the opinion.]

If there are any lingering doubts as to which advocates framed the issue(s) more effectively, they should be put to rest by the court's statement of the question in the opinion:

> The question presented for review is whether a State, consistent with the First and Fourteenth Amendments, may require a religious organization desiring to distribute and sell religious literature and to solicit donations at a state fair to conduct those activities only at an assigned location within the fairgrounds even though the application of the rule limits the religious practices of the organization.

In the first instance, of course, the selection and framing of issues are the chores of the appellant. The respondent too, however, neglects this phase of appellate work at her peril. Actions complained of by the appellant may be shown by a careful respondent to have been cured or their effects alleviated by other actions abstracted from the record. Similarly, as will be more fully explored in Chapter Three, a careful respondent will verify that the points raised by petitioner were preserved at trial, that objections were made at the appropriate time, that offers of proof were made as required and so on. Except for "plain error" (See Section 3–3), an error not preserved is not a ground for appeal.

After determining the axes upon which the appeal is to turn, the advocate must organize the argument in a way that maximizes the strength of her position. Because every case is different and every advocate is unique, there is no single structure that is universally effective. What can be said about all arguments, however—oral as well as written—is that they must have a structure if they are to be effective. An argument that meanders aimlessly from point A to point B to point W then back to point B and so on and on is doomed to fail. Although an orderly presentation is not necessarily a good presentation, a disorderly presentation is apodictically a poor one. And this is especially true when executed by and for lawyers (judges are, after all, lawyers too) who have been conditioned to orderly cognitive processes.

On the other hand, an argument with a well-defined structure permits the court to follow where the advocate wishes to lead and permits, as well, the advocate to lead it there. Moreover, it requires the advocate to determine not merely the order in which her ideas are to be presented, but also their relative importance to her position. The process of organizing the presentation of one's case requires that one make decisions about which ideas, doctrines or facts are major and which subordinate (and to which they are subordinate) as well as what arguments depend upon prior acceptance of some other position which must itself be argued. As we shall consider in greater detail later, this is of immense value in oral argument where the time for one's presentation may expand and contract with the activity of the bench, requiring the advocate constantly to shift between major points which must be made and various degrees of supporting detail or argument (See Section 8–1).

For purposes of this section we shall assume that all the preliminary research is done. (Additional supplemental research is almost always inevitable throughout one's preparation as holes appear or additional issues emerge.) We shall further assume that one is thoroughly familiar with the facts and procedural posture of the case and that the theme of the case has been at least tentatively established. It is now time to determine the structure upon which the case will rest. Obviously, that structure should support one's theme. If there is no coherent structure with which one can support the theme, the latter should be modified for it is likely to be inadequate.

Although there are a number of structural formats among which the advocate may choose, there are certain principles that are generally applicable and certain choices which must be made regardless of the particular structural mode one chooses. It will sometimes be the case, of course, that these principles will conflict in their application. At such time it is up to the advocate to determine which is to be sacrificed to which in order to present one's position in the most favorable light. If one can discover a structure that accommodates all these rhetorical principles while supporting a cogent theme, that is probably the structure of choice. It will rarely be helpful to do as one lawyer before the Supreme Court is reported (by Chief Justice Taft) to have done: to divide the argument into three parts. "In the first, I shall state the relevant facts; next, I shall propound the applicable principles of law; and, third, I shall make a lunge at the passions of the Court." Morison, *Oral Argument of Appeals*, 10 Wash. & Lee L.Rev. 1, 2 (1953).

Everything else being equal, one should lead from strength: present the strongest argument first. The selection of one's strongest argument is itself dependent upon the criteria one employs to determine relative strength. For example, one argument may have greater emotional appeal than another while the other is more cogent in terms of pre-existing legal doctrine. In such instances the choice will often depend upon the nature of the theme which the advocate has selected.

A similar choice must sometimes be made with respect to the narrowness or breadth of the position the advocate seeks to advance. This question subsumes two distinct choices. First, on what ground should the case rest in those instances in which a number of facts are relevant to the decision one is seeking. That is, should facts, arguments or issues be grouped, in which case the result sought is likely to be narrow; or should they be treated as independent grounds, any one of which would require the result the advocate wishes to achieve, in which case the result sought is likely to be broader (or, of course, some combination of these two extremes)? One's choice on this question is quite likely to be influenced by the nature of the interest one is representing. An individual party may care only about the result in the particular case. An institutional party, on the other hand—an insurance company, a government agency, a manufacturer that may have to face many other similar yet distinct claims—may have a far greater interest in a more comprehensive ruling, even if less favorable; there is often an advantage in certainty.

Second, ought one to progress from the broader argument to the narrower one or from the narrow to the broad? In what order, for example, ought one to argue that a particular state regulation is clearly unconstitutional, however and to

[22]

whomever applied, as opposed to the argument that the regulation cannot constitutionally be applied to this party on some combination of the facts presented in the particular case? Again, there is no universally correct answer to that question. Typically, a narrowly focused argument has more persuasive force than one staking out a more grandiose position. Yet if the broader argument precedes the narrower one, it may make the latter even more persuasive than it might otherwise have been by providing an intellectual set in the minds of the court that may make it more responsive to the narrower position. The narrower position may appear more reasonable, and hence more acceptable, when compared to a more sweeping, even if otherwise desirable, alternative.

Related to the question whether one ought to proceed from a broad based argument to a narrower one or vice-versa, is the question of the hierarchical level of doctrine from which one ought to proceed. In many cases an advocate may be able to argue, for example, that a regulation issued by a particular agency is not authorized by the agency's charter or that it conflicts with a state statute or violates the state constitution or is preempted by federal legislation or violates the United States Constitution. Obviously, such a progression increases the magnitude of the doctrinal issue to be determined. The questions for the advocate are at what level in this hierarchy to begin and in what direction to proceed. In general, it is probably best to begin at the lowest level of the hierarchy at which one can obtain the relief sought. Although, obviously, the advocate's choice might be influenced by the court before which the case is to be presented, most courts prefer to avoid rendering decisions on grounds of greater magnitude than necessary.

For similar reasons issue-avoidance devices should usually be presented before the issue to which they are addressed. Thus, in a case in which the issue is a party's entitlement to a jury trial, one might argue that the statute on which the claim is based provides for trial by jury before arguing that the seventh amendment to the Constitution guarantees that right; moreover, one might point out to the court that resting a favorable (though not an unfavorable) decision on the statutory ground would obviate the necessity for a decision of the constitutional question. Similarly, in those instances in which one would prefer to forestall decision of an issue, procedural irregularities that could operate to bar review— the failure of one's opponent to preserve the point for appeal by making a proper record and inadequate factual findings are but two examples— ought to precede the argument on the merits.

Finally, one needs to consider the organization of a case involving both substantive and process-oriented issues; that is, how ought one to structure a case in which the question involves not merely the outcome but the method to be used in determining that outcome? Among the substantive issues that may arise in a particular case, there often lurk questions of the appropriate standard under which to consider resolving them. For example, in reviewing the decision of a trial court, one may argue not merely that a particular result was correct but also that it was decided as a matter of fact rather than law, so that the appellate court, before it may reverse, must find not only that it disagrees with that result but also that the result is "clearly erroneous." Similarly, in arguing the unconstitutionality of a statute, one may also wish to argue that the statute must be subjected to strict scrutiny or be justified by a compelling state interest in order to pass constitutional muster. In short, one sometimes needs to argue not only what the correct result of a test is, but also what constitutes the test itself.

A similar sort of problem arises when the issue to be decided requires the interpretation of language in a legally operative instrument: contract, regulation, statute or constitution. It is often helpful to argue not merely that particular words mean a particular thing but also that those words should be interpreted in accordance with a particular theory of interpretation. Often, of course, after arguing for a particular test or theory of interpretation, the advocate will attempt to demonstrate that the result is the same regardless of the stringency of the standard employed.

In any event, what is critical here is that the issues to be argued be carefully selected and organized and that the points to be made be so structured as to maximize their persuasive force in supporting the theme of the argument. Thus, whatever other choices are to be made in terms of the rhetorical criteria we have just considered, the primary goal must be analytic coherence. No set of artificial standards can substitute for an argument structured to make sense. Consequently, the guidelines and considerations suggested here must be taken in the context of that more important goal. It is, ultimately, the content of the argument that should have the greatest impact on its structure. Only in this way can the integrity of the argument be maintained. In performing these tasks the advocate must bear in mind the nature of appellate review generally, the nature of the particular court before whom she is arguing and the kind of case being argued. All influence the sort of argument an effective advocate will make. It is to these factors that the next three chapters are devoted.

CHAPTER THREE

THE APPELLATE PROCESS

§ 3–1. An Overview

In a general sense all advocacy, at whatever level of the judicial hierarchy, is similar; it is persuasion. Yet the problems of the appellate advocate differ in important respects from those of her colleague at the trial level because of differences in the appellate process itself. Thus, to understand better the job of the appellate advocate and to appreciate the nature of her craft—to be able to persuade effectively in an appellate court —requires an understanding of the appellate process.

Some form of reconsideration of decisions is an important part of legal systems and all American jurisdictions provide at least one level of appellate review. Of course, there may be different models of review. A reviewing court, for example, may simply repeat the process undertaken by the original tribunal—*i.e.*, may try the case *de novo*, taking evidence in order to maximize the likelihood of discovering "truth." This procedure, followed by the ecclesiastical courts, was rejected by the American colonies (although some American jurisdictions still employ *de novo* review by courts of general jurisdiction over courts whose jurisdiction is limited, generally to lesser claims or offenses).

The model adopted in America and the predominant model still employed today was developed from the common law writ of error. Appeal by writ of error is not a rehearing of the case but a review of the record to determine the existence of some mistake made during the original proceeding. Thus, the appellate process is not designed or intended to give the litigants a second bite of the apple. It is rather a necessary corrective for errors committed at trial that may have affected the decision there made. The purpose of an appeal is to correct errors of law. The task of the appellant is to convince the court that the judge below made a mistake.

Virtually all trials are zero sum games. To the extent that one party wins, another loses. The losing party of course may feel somewhat disgruntled by the result of the trial. If the dissatisfaction is sufficiently strong and the likelihood of success sufficiently great, the losing party may well appeal to a higher court. Rarely, however, is the basis of this appeal the erroneousness of the result reached at trial. It is rather that the process used in arriving at this result was somehow flawed or tainted by some error of law. Thus, one way of viewing the appellate process is as a trial of the trial—the appellant complaining that she was the victim and suffered injury as a result of some error or errors committed by the trial judge and the appellee taking the position that either no error was committed or that any such error did not affect the result.

The party taking the appeal (the appellant or petitioner) must follow certain formalities if her case is to be heard by a higher court. Although the formalities differ from jurisdiction to jurisdiction, certain generalizations can be made. Typically, although subject to a number of exceptions, only final judgments are appealable; interlocutory orders may not be appealed. This rule operates to save the judicial system from the inefficiencies of piecemeal (and perhaps unnecessary) litigation. A party dissatisfied with some action of the trial court must await the conclusion of the trial process and only then—and only if she has been hurt by the adverse ruling—collect all her complaints and make them in a single proceeding.

There are generally time limits during which an appeal must be taken. The time begins to run with the entry of judgment by the trial court and the failure to proceed in a timely fashion is ordinarily fatal to the appeal. Assuming that the appeal has been timely filed the next step is the transmission of the record (or more frequently that portion of the record necessary to a decision) to the appellate court. This requires an agreement among counsel on what is to be included and must also be done within the time prescribed by statute or rule.

Similarly, briefs must be filed within the time permitted and must conform to the form requirements of the court. Petitioner's brief is first filed, followed by respondent's brief, followed (in most courts) by a reply brief. In many academic moot court exercises, briefs are exchanged simultaneously and reply briefs are not permitted. This departure from the real world of appellate practice has some effect on the way the briefs are prepared (see Chapter Seven).

After the submission of briefs the court will schedule a time for oral argument. (Some courts in some cases may decide the case "on the briefs," *i.e.*, without hearing oral argument.) Occasionally, supplemental memoranda may be filed after oral argument. The court will then take the case under advisement and sometime thereafter render its decision, although on occasion the court may announce its decision from the bench immediately. There may then be a further appeal to a still higher court. In many jurisdictions this second appeal is discretionary; that is, the litigant must persuade the court that his cause is worthy of additional review. Typically, the decision to grant such review is based more on the importance of the issue than on the merits of the particular case.

The appellate process differs from the trial process in a number of particulars. Typically, the goal of the trial is as much to determine historical facts as it is to declare or apply legal principles. Appellate courts by contrast are concerned almost entirely with the declaration or application of legal principles. Moreover, in many instances, the legal principles with which the appellate court is concerned will have substantially greater impact than merely deciding the case immediately before the court. It is far less usual for this to be true of a trial court's decision. And, of course, the higher the court the more likely is this to be true.

§ 3–2. Limits on Appellate Power: Standards of Review

In the common law system appellate review is not a second trial—not a rehearing of the evidence or, in the usual case, a search for truth. It is, rather, a review of the record for errors committed during the pre-trial and trial stages. Thus, the facts are rarely re-examined (although whether the facts found are sufficient to support the judgment may be). Consequently the appellate advocate has less of an opportunity than her trial colleague to shape the case. The raw materials with which she must work are limited to legal authority and the frozen record of the trial. It is what the advocate can make of these materials that will determine the effectiveness of her presentation.

Because the appeal is not a second trial but an examination of the first one, it is on the actions of the trial judge that the advocate must focus. Yet not all actions of the trial court are judged by the same standards. For example, in addition to ruling on disputed legal issues, trial judges must also determine questions of fact. Sometimes these factual determinations are a necessary predicate to a ruling on some issue of law, as when the admissibility of evidence depends upon some antecedent factual determination. For example, a judge called upon to determine whether a weapon is admissible over a claim that it is the fruit of an unlawful search may have to decide whether the arresting officer's testimony that the weapon was in plain view, or the defendant's testimony that it was not, more accurately reflects what happened. The legal ruling on admissibility cannot be made until the facts are decided. Sometimes these factual determinations are made by the court as if by a jury. If the parties have elected a bench trial, the judge must decide questions of ultimate fact as well as determining the legal significance of these facts once found.

In either instance, the trial judge's findings of fact are not subject to the same sort of review as her purely legal rulings. The reasons should be plain. The trial judge will have seen and heard the witnesses; the appellate court is restricted to a printed transcript. The trial judge will have presided over the entire proceeding enabling her to gain a "feel" for the case that although ethereal is nonetheless important and, again, impossible to duplicate in a transcript. Consequently, the trial court is in a far better position than the appellate court to determine factual issues and the trial court's findings with respect to such issues are owed a great deal of deference. The standard of review for such findings, whether denominated "clearly erroneous," "without support in the record" or by some similar catch phrase, is substantially higher than the standard for purely legal questions. (In those cases in which the trial court is not in a substantially better position as fact-finder than the appellate court—where, for example, the case turns on documentary evidence equally available to the reviewing court—the latter's examination is likely to be more far-ranging though the nominal standard remains the same.)

Even with respect to questions of law, however, there is more than a single standard governing review of the trial court's decisions. The determination of many issues likely to arise during the course of a trial are within the trial court's "discretion." Such rulings will not be reversed unless there has been "an abuse of discretion." What these labels signify is simply that the party seeking a reversal based on such a ruling has a substantially greater burden. The sorts of issues which call forth this appellate deference are again, in the main, those about which presence at the trial is an important source of information. For example, many evidentiary rulings depend upon a balancing of the probative value of the proffered evidence against any prejudicial effect it is likely to have on the trier of fact. The trial judge has observed the participants, including the jury, and is aware of the entire context in which the evidence will be considered. Moreover, she may be more familiar with the dynamics of trials generally than the judges of an appellate court. Consequently, she is typically in a better position to evaluate the factors relevant to the decision. Similarly, the decisions on motions to declare a mistrial, or for a new trial or motions to strike evidence are likely to be governed by the abuse of discretion standard. Once that label attaches, reversal will be more difficult to obtain, although how much more difficult varies from case to case and from court to court.

Consequently, the party seeking to reverse a trial court's ruling will frequently argue that what may appear to be a finding of fact or a discretionary ruling is really simply a decision on some straightforward legal issue. Such an argument, if successful, permits the appellate court to reverse on a determination that the lower court was merely wrong, rather than clearly wrong. The determination of purely legal issues does not require either an intimate knowledge of trial dynamics nor any special sensitivity to the events or context of the particular trial. Hence, the appellate court is in at least as good a position as the trial judge to render such decisions. Moreover, the collegial nature of appellate courts, at least in theory, makes it more likely that a just result will be reached. Even with respect to the purely legal decision, however, there is an inertial force that the party seeking reversal of a trial judge's ruling must overcome. After all, at least one judge has already ruled that the law is otherwise than the advocate claims it to be. Judges do not lightly reverse their colleagues.

Indeed, even if some error has been committed, reversal will be problematic if it is unlikely that the error contributed to the judgment from which the appeal is taken. To the extent that the result would have been the same regardless of the claimed error there is little reason to reverse. A trial of any length or complexity is unlikely to be entirely free of error; thus, the necessity of the various escape devices to avoid the otherwise perpetual trial and reversal and retrial of cases. These devices, however—the law/fact distinction, discretionary rulings, the harmless error notion —limit the range of action that can be asked of an appellate court. Hence, the appellate advocate must plan accordingly.

§ 3–3. Limits on Appellate Power: The Record

The record comprises the pleadings, pre-trial motions, transcript (a verbatim account taken by a court stenographer) of the testimony, objections and rulings at the trial, including requests to charge the jury, the exhibits entered into evidence, post-trial motions and any colloquy between court and counsel not held "off the record." The record, or those parts of it agreed to by counsel as representing the basis for the appeal, must be filed with the appellate court.

In addition to freezing the facts, the record presents a further hurdle to the party seeking a reversal based on some action of the trial court. With but two exceptions (about which more in a moment), an advocate may not raise a point on appeal unless that point has been "preserved." What this means is that the claimed error must have been called to the attention of the trial court so that the opportunity to take corrective action was present. The rationale is that in many cases the need for an appeal would thereby be obviated and that the failure to raise the point operates as a waiver. Thus, a claim that evidence was erroneously admitted at trial will not be heard on appeal unless a timely objection had been made to permit the trial court either to exclude the evidence or to strike it. Similarly, a claim that the jury had been improperly instructed will not be entertained unless an objection was made at a point in the trial that would permit the trial court to correct any errors.

At one time the process of making the record was a trap for the unwary, requiring the careful observance of certain formalities. For example, an objection to the admission of evidence was not, in most jurisdictions, sufficient to preserve the point. If the objection was overruled, it was necessary for trial counsel to except to the ruling. If counsel failed to take an exception the objection would be deemed abandoned. Fortunately, such formality is no longer necessary in most jurisdictions. Nonetheless, a mere objection, without more, may still be insufficient to preserve the point for appeal. What is required in most jurisdictions today is a statement of the reasons for the objection that will permit the trial court to make an informed decision on the question. The so-called general objection, unless the basis for it is obvious, will not do. The appellate court will treat the objection for which no grounds are advanced as though no objection had been made.

Where the claimed error lies not in admitting evidence over objection but in excluding evidence that it is claimed should have been admitted, more is required to make the record. In those situations, in addition to advancing grounds for the admission of the evidence, it is also necessary to make some showing of the nature of the evidence. This is called an "offer of proof" and it serves two functions. First, it enables the trial court to make an informed decision with respect to the proferred evidence. Second, and equally important, it permits the appellate court to make an informed decision; if no offer of proof is made on the record, the appellate court is without knowledge of the substance of the evidence. It cannot tell either whether it was error to exclude it or, if it was, whether the error was likely to contribute significantly to the judgment being appealed.

The same sort of action is required to preserve other than evidentiary points. For example, a claim that a particular instruction should not have been given to the jury can be preserved by objection (including the grounds on which it is based) before the jury begins to deliberate; a claim that the trial judge failed to give a particular instruction, on the other hand, requires that trial counsel have made a timely request for that instruction on the record. It is then the trial court's refusal to give the requested instruction that forms the ground of the appeal.

It is through the jury instructions and the pleadings that the substantive law governing the parties' rights and defenses enters the case.

Thus, any basis for appeal that relies on these substantive grounds—that is, not based upon the admission or exclusion of evidence because of technical rules of evidence nor based on procedural irregularities—must be rooted in claims made at the trial. Yet this may make difficult one of the more important functions of the appellate process. As we shall see in the next chapter, appellate courts play a dual role. First, they must correct the errors committed by trial courts in order to do justice between the parties to particular cases. Second, however, they are also largely responsible for the development and growth of the law. It is this second role that can become problematic because of the necessity of preserving points to be raised on appeal. If, for example, appellate counsel wishes to argue that the long standing rule in the jurisdiction that acceptance of an offer is effective when sent should be changed so that acceptances are effective only upon receipt, the likelihood that the appellate court will accept the argument is diminished if the point was not raised at trial. Yet, because trial courts are bound by prior decisions of the courts superior to them, trial counsel often forego raising such issues—even in the unlikely event it occurs to them.

The point for appellate counsel, of course, is that the difficulty of obtaining a change in the law is compounded by the failure to seek such change at the trial level. Often, therefore, an argument that prior decisions should be narrowed or overruled or for some other reason should not control the case *sub judice* must be advanced as an alternative ground for a claim of error otherwise supported. Appellate counsel must be alert to discover the peg—the preserved point—upon which to hang her argument for a modification of existing doctrine.

Although the general rule, applied in the overwhelming majority of cases, is that an appellate court will not consider points that had not first been presented to the trial court, there are rare —very rare—occasions upon which a reversal may be made on grounds raised for the first time on appeal. One such category, questions of jurisdiction, we will consider in the next section. Apart from questions going to the court's power to decide, however, there are instances in which the trial court has committed error so palpable that the appellate court will reverse although trial counsel neglected to preserve the point.

This exception, the "plain error" doctrine, might be viewed as a safety net for those unusual instances in which all the participants at trial charged with protecting the rights of the parties have blundered in some substantial way. Theoretically, the policy underlying the need for calling the point to the trial court's attention is satisfied by the obviousness of the error; that is, it can be said that the claimed error was so palpable that the trial court should have been aware of it even in the absence of an objection. The secondary justification for making the record—that waiver of the point, or acquiescence in the trial court's action or failure to act, may be inferred from the failure to make a timely objection—is obviously artificial in the plain error situation. One might speculate about whether the plain error doctrine serves to protect counsel from liability for inadequate representation as often as it protects parties from becoming victims of errors that go beyond the point of permissible standards of practice.

The worst situation for the advocate is the case in which the only ground for appeal rests upon a claim of plain error. For in that situation the court can dispose of the entire case by invoking the failure to make the record. Where there are independent grounds for appeal and the plain error notion is used as a device to persuade the court to consider additional points, the going may be somewhat easier. If the plain error notion must be relied upon, it is perhaps most effective where it is closely connected to claims of error that had been preserved. In some jurisdictions, for example, it is necessary to submit requests to charge the jury in order to argue on appeal that there was error in the judge's instructions and it is also necessary to object to the instructions giv-

en to the extent they depart from those requested. If trial counsel has satisfied the first requirement but not the second, it may be somewhat
easier to invoke plain error on appeal.

As one might imagine, the plain error doctrine
is not a very satisfactory basis upon which to
rest an appeal. It is difficult to emphasize sufficiently how heavy the burden is upon the advocate who seeks to raise an issue for the first time
at the appellate level. She must persuade the
court not merely that there was error but that
that error was so palpable, so clearly injurious to
the validity of the judgment from which the appeal is taken as to require virtually automatic reversal. Thus, the advocate must persuade the
court that it should consider the claim at the
very same time that she is seeking to advance a
particular result of that consideration. Obviously, it is far more difficult to integrate two different levels of argument—that there was error and
that the failure to assert it ought not bar appellate consideration and reversal—than to argue
simply that there was reversible error.

§ 3–4. Limits on Appellate Power: Jurisdiction

There is one category of issue that may be
raised for the first time on appeal without running into the difficulties presented by having to
argue plain error. It is that category of cases in
which the claim is advanced that the court lacks

power to consider the case—that it is without subject matter jurisdiction. Thus, there are two differences between an appellate court's refusal to hear a case based upon the failure to preserve the point on which the appeal is taken and the refusal to entertain it based upon a lack of jurisdiction. First, the latter is categorical; it is concerned with only one kind of issue. Second, and for the advocate more important, it is at least nominally unconnected with the underlying merits of the substantive issues.

Because the question of subject matter jurisdiction deals with the power of the court to act, it is not susceptible to the control of the parties. The law of subject matter jurisdiction reflects concerns having to do with the court's relationship to other organs of society rather than to the individual litigants in the particular case. Thus, personal jurisdiction—the power of a court over the parties to a case—can be conferred by the parties while subject matter jurisdiction cannot. Just as the parties cannot confer subject matter jurisdiction so the failure to object to its exercise does not foreclose the issue. Indeed, courts at any level of the judicial hierarchy are said to be obliged to raise the issue *sua sponte*. Even the party first invoking a court's jurisdiction may challenge it later in the proceedings.

The question of subject matter jurisdiction is a trap for the unwary advocate. Hence, the wise advocate will be certain of the source of the court's power. For an appellate court this involves two inquiries: First, is there power to hear the case in the judicial system of which the appellate court is a part; and, second, is there jurisdiction in the particular appellate court. The first is primarily the concern of the party that prevailed below because a lack of power in the system requires a finding that the actions of the inferior court are of no effect. Thus, the judgment won is a nullity. The second is primarily the concern of the appellant because lack of appellate power entails the inability of the court to act upon the decision below. Thus, the judgment below must stand.

A systemic lack of jurisdiction might exist either because the claim is one not cognizable in any court—a non-justiciable dispute—or because some other judicial system has the exclusive power to resolve the controversy. Claims may be non-justiciable for any one of a number of reasons: the dispute is not ripe for judicial resolution; there is a lack of standing to litigate the claim; the case is moot; the questions presented are political in nature and committed to another branch of government. Regardless of any other issues that are to be raised on the appeal, if there is any question of the justiciability of the dispute the advocates must be prepared to deal with it.

Similarly, the advocates must be able to establish that no other judicial system has the exclusive power to consider the controversy. Notice that the difficulty does not arise if there is concurrent power in some other judicial system but only if the power of that other system is exclusive. For example, a case brought in federal court on the basis of diversity of citizenship is one which state courts are also likely to have power to consider. The power of the state court does not preclude a like power in federal court; the power of the federal court does not preclude a like power in state courts. On the other hand, claims for infringement of copyright or patent, for example, are committed exclusively to the federal courts. Hence, there is no power in the state courts to entertain a case arising under the federal statute protecting those property rights. The power of courts to exercise the judicial function is limited by constitution and by statute. Failure to meet the requirements imposed by either necessitates dismissal of the case.

Assuming that the controversy is appropriate for judicial resolution and that the court system in which the case was brought has power to hear it, it is still necessary to establish the power of the particular appellate court. Each judicial system imposes its own requirements on the particular courts within it. Some cases may be reviewable only in a particular court; some may be reviewable as a matter of discretion; some may not be reviewable at all. It is necessary to verify that one is in the correct forum and that all the requirements for appellate review in that forum have been met.

As we have noted, what is peculiar about jurisdictional issues is that they are treated as if they were independent of the merits of the underlying substantive questions. The policy bases concern the role of courts, the role of this court, the appellate process, judicial efficiency and similar values. Yet, there are times when an advocate may be able to play off a strong case on the merits, especially if it appeals to the sense of justice, against what might otherwise be jurisdictional impediments. Such arguments are especially attractive where, for example, a denial of jurisdiction would eliminate the possibility of any relief, where there is no other available forum.

In such instances, the value of a limiting principle ought to be obvious; it permits the court to reach the merits of this case without opening the floodgates to superficially similar cases. Indeed, in the somewhat different context already considered this may be one of the functions of the plain error doctrine: it permits an appellate court to deal with the egregious situation while preserving, in the more typical case, the requirement of making the record.

Problems of jurisdiction are simply one category of procedural issues. The discussion, therefore, on the procedural case (Section 5–2) is equally applicable to cases that call into question the very power of the court to act. What is crucial to recognize here is that jurisdictional issues may be raised without warning by the court on its own motion or by one's adversary even if she were the party originally invoking the court's jurisdiction. Thus, it is a matter about which the advocate must always be prepared.

§ 3–5. Multi-Judge Panels

Perhaps the most striking physical difference between the trial court and the appellate court is the number of judges that participate in the decisionmaking process. Trials, of course, are typically presided over by a single judge. Appeals, on the other hand, are heard and decided by panels usually consisting of at least three judges. In the Supreme Court nine Justices participate in the cases presented. Some appellate cases may be heard and decided by a still greater number.

This facet of the appellate process, as well as those already discussed, operates to limit, at least as a practical matter, the power of the appellate court. Collegiality requires that the members of the court discuss and argue the case among themselves; but it requires something more as well: It requires that a majority of the court reach agreement on an appropriate disposition. Moreover, while more than agreement in the ultimate result may not be required, appellate judges usually strive to accommodate the views of their colleagues in the opinion written in support of the disposition of the appeal. This need to compromise is also in part responsible for the gradualness with which the common law changes.

This felt need to obtain the agreement (or at least the acquiescence) of other members of the court is in part responsible for the apparent homogenization and amalgamation of notions sometimes found in majority opinons. Dissenting or concurring opinions, on the other hand, often representing the views only of the author, frequently demonstrate a much cleaner and hence stronger stylistic and analytic line.

The collegial processes of argument and accommodation, indeed, the decisionmaking process itself as well as the writing of the opinion that memorializes, explains and justifies the disposition —all of this occurs out of the presence and without the direct participation of the advocate. Her only involvement at these crucial times is through what the participating judges are willing to accept and use of her earlier submitted contribution. Thus, one of the goals of the effective advocate is to present an argument that will be useful and appropriate intellectual ammunition for a favorable judge to use in trying to convince her colleagues.

The most effective presentations so directed may find their way into the opinion of the court. It is a useful exercise to compare well-executed appellate arguments (oral or written) with the courts' opinions in those cases. Presentations that can be easily incorporated into the opinion of the court are the kind of presentations likely to prevail. They justify a result without the appearance of strident partisanship.

The requirement of written opinions justifying particular results through reasoned elaboration of legal doctrine is otherwise significant as well. The advocate preparing an argument for an appellate court does so with a particular kind of audience in view. There are characteristics of thought and approach common to most judicial minds that the advocate ignores at her peril. Any argument is likely to be more persuasive if designed with its intended recipients in view. But the advocate typically knows more than the kind of audience to which she must address her presentation; often she knows or can discover a good deal about the individual members of that audience by examining earlier opinions written by the judges who are to decide her case.

(There are times when the advocate will not know the particular judges who will make up the court at the time for submission of briefs. In the federal courts of appeals, for example, there are floating three-judge panels selected from among the composition of the whole court. Even in such cases, however, the advocate will often be able to predict at least some of the members of the panel. And, of course, by the time of oral argument the composition of the panel will be known.)

If the identities of the decisionmakers are known, it is foolish not to acquire whatever information might be helpful in casting an argument designed to persuade those individuals. Although we are a government of laws, those laws are applied and interpreted through the wisdom of human judges; a responsible advocate seeks to appeal to the individual manifestation of that wisdom in particular decisionmakers. Thus, the advocate should take the time to read the judicial opinions and other writings of the judges at least as they pertain to the issues presented by the appeal. Expressions of the judges' views with respect to larger questions are also often helpful. One can at least get a feel for the style and quality of the minds to whom one must address one's case. So, for example, a judge concerned about issues of federalism might be shown that the result for which the advocate contends will not interfere unduly with the exercise of state sovereignty, while one devoted to the expansion of individual rights will be more likely to be persuad-

[50]

ed by a demonstration of the necessity of a particular result to their protection. At the very least, such knowledge enables the advocate to determine that she cannot ignore certain consequences or implications of her position without imperiling her case. One does not lightly suggest to a court whose members are sensitive to the appropriate division of power between the legislative and judicial branches that the consequences of a particular decision to that balance are of no concern—at least not if one expects to persuade.

There are cases in which it will be evident that of, say, a seven person court, perhaps two judges will agree with the advocate's position based on their prior opinions, while perhaps two more can be predicted to disagree. The advocate may in such circumstances pitch her argument to the remaining three judges who, as a practical matter, will be likely to decide the case. Care must be taken, of course, not to alienate the relatively safe votes nor to appear to take them for granted. In fact, it is for these judges that the advocate needs to supply the arguments and marshall the facts and authorities for use in the conference room, so that they can convince their colleagues.

One final word of caution is in order: The advocate must not be too hasty in either taking for granted sure votes in her favor or crossing off apparently certain votes against her position.

The practice of ascribing positions to judges in a case not yet decided based on the views they have elsewhere expressed can lead to quite unpleasant surprises.

CHAPTER FOUR

LEVELS OF REVIEW

It should be obvious that the role of an appellate court differs significantly from that of a trial court. Less obvious, but nonetheless true, is that there are differences in the roles to be performed by different kinds of appellate courts. These differences have to do with the balance to be struck between the two functions of all appellate courts: (1) to decide the concrete disputes before them —that is, whether error so tainted a trial as to require reversal; and (2) to declare the law in order to guide the future behavior both of citizens and of lower courts.

The importance for the advocate of the differences in focus from one kind of appellate court to another is plain. One might argue very differently to a court that viewed its responsibility as being principally to the parties than one might to a court that viewed its responsibility as being principally to the integrity of the law system. It is important to note, however, that these two roles are not mutually exclusive; in fact, they are often complementary. Moreover, the differences among various appellate courts with respect to this issue are more differences in focus or emphasis than radical differences in fundamental approach.

Nevertheless, there are differences and they are important to the advocate.

§ 4-1. State Intermediate Appellate Courts

All state judicial systems provide at least one level of appellate review. In those states the appellate court must serve both of the functions just considered. Many states, however, have a multi-tiered system of review. Typically, the highest court in such a system exercises a discretionary jurisdiction while the intermediate courts' jurisdiction is mandatory. As a consequence, the intermediate court reviews many more cases, and is concerned more with achieving the correct result in the particular cases before it than in reforming the law of the jurisdiction.

Because these courts provide the first review of the trial court's actions, they are systemically inclined to focus more narrowly than courts superior to them on the particulars of the case. Moreover, as a practical matter, for most litigants there will be no further review and, as a result, justice in the particular case may be of overriding concern. Finally, because of the volume of cases, there may be less time for the sort of reflection helpful to sound policy-making by the judiciary.

Superior courts exist to consider whether sweeping—or not so sweeping—changes in the legal doctrine of the jurisdiction should be made or whether established doctrine should be preserved. The existence of higher courts naturally inhibits law-making in the intermediate courts in two ways. First, the ultimate judicial responsibility for the state's law rests elsewhere, making it relatively painless for the intermediate appellate courts to default on this aspect of the appellate function. It is also the case, however, that the intermediate appellate courts are bound by the earlier pronouncements of the courts above them in the judicial hierarchy. To fail to adhere to these decisions is to fail to fulfill the responsibilities of their office as well as to invite reversal.

To a considerable degree these factors influence the sorts of arguments that are likely to be effective before such tribunals. First, because the primary role of the intermediate court is to do justice between the parties the particular facts are of critical importance. It is the facts disclosed by the record and the inferences to be drawn from those facts that are far more likely to impel decision than more broad jurisprudential notions or policy based arguments. The implication for the advocate is to keep her argument concrete and relatively case specific. Consistent with this, procedural niceties are likely to be more significant in the appellate court closest in the judicial hierarchy to the trial. Thus, it is especially important to guard against procedural impediments and to be prepared to deal with procedural arguments.

Just as significant for the advocate as the immediacy of the relationship between the intermediate appellate court and the trial court is the relationship between the intermediate appellate court and the state's highest court. Inferior courts are bound by the decisions of superior courts in the same system. Intermediate appellate courts cannot question the validity of decisions rendered by the courts of last resort within their jurisdiction. Such decisions are controlling authority, in some respects similar to statutory provisions applicable to a case. Thus the advocate must be aware not only of the decisions of the court before which she is appearing, but also of those courts superior to it. Difficult as it is to prevail upon a court to overturn one of its own decisions, it is still arguable; one may not argue, however, that an intermediate court should overturn the decisions of a higher court.

Consider, for example, the case of a child badly injured by a neighbor's five German shepherds when the child climbed a chainlink fence and entered their yard. If the cause of action arose in a state where the common law affords only minimal protection to trespassers, even very young ones, and the trial court awarded summary judgment to the dog owners, the intermediate level appellate court is not the place to argue for a

change in the state's outmoded law of trespass.
Rather, the argument would focus on how this
case does not fall squarely within existing
precedent. To do that effectively, the advocate
must read *every* case on injured trespassers decided in the jurisdiction and be able to distinguish them from the case at bar on the facts.
(The number and breed of dogs might be significant as would the locus delecti: keeping more
than one "inherently dangerous animal" on resi-
dential property.) Once that has been done, the
advocate may certainly make the policy argument (i.e., that the law should be changed); but
it is, at this point in the appellate process, only
supportive of and subordinate to an argument
based on existing law.

Whether a particular decision of a superior
court controls the outcome in the intermediate
court depends upon the similarity of the cases.
Hence, it is always open to the advocate to argue
that a decision claimed to control is distinguishable or that the case is controlled by a different
decision leading to a contrary result. There are
thus three possible positions that may obtain in
any case in which the effects of decisions of superior on inferior courts is concerned: First, it may
be claimed that there is binding authority favoring one of the parties; second, it may be claimed
that there is no binding authority; finally it may

be claimed that there is binding authority favoring the other party.

Obviously, each party would like to claim that controlling authority supports her position. Sometimes both parties can proffer such arguments. Where the case before the intermediate court falls between two stools, each leaning in a direction opposite to the other, each advocate is likely to argue that the case is closer to this one or closer to that one and that the earlier decision upon which she relies controls. If the court accepts her interpretation of the authority, the advocate prevails.

It is essential in arguing a case to an intermediate appellate court to be able to analyze the decisions binding that court in a way that, if they do not compel a result in one's favor, at least do not compel a result in one's adversary's favor. Each advocate will attempt to show that the decision relied upon by her adversary is distinguishable from the case being argued.

It may be that each advocate will persuade the court that the cases relied upon by the other are inapposite or distinguishable. It is important to recognize, however, that demonstrating that authority does not compel a result against one's position is quite different from demonstrating that one ought to prevail. It is the difference between compulsion and freedom: That the court *need* not reach a particular result does not say that it *should* not.

Even in such cases—cases in which the intermediate court is not bound by higher authority —the advocate is better advised to argue that the result for which she contends fits more comfortably into the existing fabric of the state's jurisprudence than to attempt to blaze new trails. Analogies to decisions already rendered and reliance upon the principles underlying those decisions are likely to be more effective than simply pressing one's position as the better view.

In part this results from another role of the intermediate appellate court: translator and transmitter of the notions of the court of last resort to the trial courts of the jurisdiction. Because courts of last resort speak to relatively fewer issues than the intermediate appellate courts, it is in part up to the latter to determine how the pronouncements of the superior court are to be applied to cases of greater or lesser similarity to those that gave rise to the pronouncements. This is an especially important function in the federal judicial system and we shall return to it in Section 4–3. For now, however, it is sufficient to note that counsel will often argue from the implications or direction of higher authority as well as from the precise decisions.

In short, the basic difference for the advocate between intermediate and final appellate courts is that there is one argument that may be appropriate for the latter but not generally for the former: the argument that an earlier decision of a court of last resort ought not be followed. The only significant exception is the argument that the higher court has itself effectively, though not explicitly, overruled its own earlier decision by refusing to follow or apply it in substantially similar cases. Such an approach is likely to be most successful where the need to guide trial courts in interpreting apparently conflicting pronouncements by the court of last resort is especially strong.

§ 4–2. State Courts of Last Resort

There are a number of important differences between intermediate appellate courts and state courts of last resort to which the effective advocate must be sensitive. Perhaps the primary difference is the extent to which the higher court attends its role as involving something more or other than merely doing justice between the particular parties by correcting errors committed at trial. In a multi-tiered appellate system there will already have been a review of claimed errors. Further review so narrowly focused is not likely to add to a correct result at anything approaching the frequency appropriate to justify the cost.

Thus, these courts sit for reasons other than the correction of error. This is also reflected in the jurisdictional bases of many courts of last resort. Typically, the jurisdiction of intermediate courts is mandatory; the courts must decide all those cases that it is empowered to decide. In many state judicial systems the jurisdiction of courts of last resort, by contrast, is discretionary; these courts may pick and choose from among the cases brought before them those they wish to hear. The others they may refuse to hear. The correctness of the decision below is only occasionally a significant criterion of selection. Rather, the criteria of choice include the importance of the issue to be decided, inconsistent decisions in the lower courts within the judicial system, the need for certainty, the need to resolve an issue of first impression or the need to determine whether a change in existing doctrine is desirable.

These criteria suggest a shift in the emphasis with which the court views its dual roles. As one moves upward through the judicial hierarchy the importance of correcting error tends to diminish and the public institutional role—that of guiding the development of the law within the jurisdiction—takes on increasing importance. It should be noted, however, that this is a change only in focus, in what the court views as more important and less important. It is not to suggest that the facts of the case are regarded as unimportant.

Consider, for example, the case of the young trespasser related in the previous section. If, as seems likely, the intermediate appellate court has affirmed the trial court's dismissal of the plaintiff's claim and the state's court of last resort has agreed to consider the case, it is there that the advocate might argue for a change in the law. Now is the time to bring to bear on the argument all those moving and equitable points about the need for exceptions because of the number of young children in a family-type community, the antiquated nature of the present law, the changes wrought by urbanization, and anything else that the advocate's fertile legal imagination can produce.

As can be seen, the treatment accorded the facts by the advocate arguing to a court of last resort should reflect the differences in the court's role. To some extent this will occur naturally as the case wends its way up the judicial ladder. Each level of appeal acts as a filter, as it were, that often results in a loss of fine detail. The "facts" of a trial often become the "situation" with which a court of last resort must deal. Indeed, there have been instances in which the complexion of a case, the sorts of issues and notions involved in it, change more or less dramatically as the case progresses from one level of the judiciary to a higher level. In the well-known *Pullman* case, a comparison of the opinion of the district court, *Pullman Co. v. Railroad Commission*, 33 F.Supp. 675 (W.D.Tex. 1940), with that of the Supreme Court, *Railroad Commission v. Pullman Co.*, 312 U.S. 496, 61 S.Ct. 643 (1941), furnishes an instructive example. The Supreme Court was concerned with the substantial constitutional issue presented under the equal protection clause of the fourteenth amendment, an issue neither addressed nor even noted in the opinion of the lower court.

In any event, the advocate must be sensitive to these differences in the way that the facts are important. One might emphasize, for example, that the facts are typical of a situation that requires the approach for which the advocate is contending. On the other hand, one might argue that the peculiar facts of one's case require only a minor departure from existing doctrine. Indeed, this latter argument can be quite effective in those instances in which a change of direction may be contemplated by the court although it is not entirely confident of the necessity or desirability of the change. A small step in an unusual case can provide the feedback to the court to permit it better to assess the consequences of a more dramatic change and may also serve a cueing function for lower courts within the system—to signal that change may be in the offing. Thus, in the case we have been considering, a ruling in the plaintiff's favor will be likely to suggest to lower courts in the jurisdiction that the rule limiting liability to trespassers might be more flexibly applied than it had been before the decision.

Because courts of last resort have the power to overrule their prior decisions, there are arguments available to advocates appearing before them that rarely can be used by those appearing before the intermediate courts that must answer to a superior tribunal. But to say that one can argue that prior understandings should be overturned is not to say that one should so argue. Generally, arguments that a particular doctrine has become outmoded or that question the validity of past decisions are less effective than those seeking to incorporate the sought after rule or result into the existing body of the jurisdiction's law. Forces of certainty, predictability, fairness (especially to those who may have relied upon the old rule) and, perhaps strongest of all, inertia all militate against frequent or lightly undertaken overruling of even bad decisions.

Thus, when prior cases appear adverse to one's position it is ordinarily more effective to seek a limiting decision; that is to attempt to distinguish the precedent from the case at bar, to limit its reach so that it does not require the adverse decision. In short, the advocate might argue as if to an intermediate court bound by the prior decision, but with this important qualification: The artificial distinction (as opposed to the real albeit fine one) that may serve the cueing function.

when used by the court of last resort to signal a change of direction to lower courts, is rarely appropriate in the intermediate court whose responsibilities include executing the pronouncements of a superior tribunal.

All this having been said, there are instances in which a direct attack on precedent is better practice than the oblique attempt to erode its effects. Where the advocate's position is that the adverse decision has generated a bad rule rather than that the application of the rule to the particular case will yield a bad result, it is more effective as well as more responsible to say so. Pettifogging attempts at artificial distinctions not grounded in reasoned, principled analysis dilute the integrity of the advocate's argument. The agonizing, ingenuous use of any and all devices to avoid at all costs the argument that a prior decision should be overruled is poor practice whether engaged in by courts or advocates. Much better the straight-forward appeal to reason and good sense.

Of course, with respect to federal issues over which the United States Supreme Court has the final judicial word, the state courts of last resort speak somewhat like an intermediate court. The differences are, first, that as a practical matter extraordinarily few cases will undergo further appellate review; and, second, that to the extent state issues are so intertwined with the federal as to permit the state's law to support the judgment independent of any federal ground, the state court's decision is unreviewable. Consequently, in arguing a case containing federal and state ingredients before a state court of last resort, the advocate needs to consider whether state or federal grounds should be relied upon for the result sought.

§ 4–3. Federal Courts of Appeals

With the exception of some specialized tribunals which need not concern us here, the federal courts are organized in a three-tiered system: At the lowest level in this hierarchy are the district courts, the federal trial courts; at the top is the Supreme Court of the United States (which we shall consider in the following section). Between them are the United States Courts of Appeals for the various circuits. (The nation is divided geographically into twelve circuits.)

These courts have much in common with both intermediate appellate courts and courts of last resort. They are like the former in that they provide the initial review of claims of trial error. Moreover, also like other intermediate appellate courts their own decisions are subject to review by a higher tribunal whose pronouncements, expressed through Supreme Court opinions, must be interpreted and applied. Yet, unlike intermediate appellate courts in most state systems, as a practical matter they have the final word in the over-whelming number of cases argued before them. The Supreme Court reviews exceedingly few cases decided by the courts of appeals.

With respect to one particular group of cases, the federal courts of appeals are in a most unusual if not unique posture. In cases that are in federal court because of diversity of citizenship but for which state law supplies the rule of decision under the *Erie* doctrine, the courts of appeals are required to adhere to the precedents of courts that are without power to review their decisions. Thus, for example, if the court of last resort of a state whose law governs has decided not to adopt comparative negligence, the federal court may not apply a comparative negligence theory although it believes it to be better law and although it might be free to adopt it if state law were not controlling. Yet, if it misconstrues, erodes or evades governing state law, there is little that can be done; the state courts, even the state court of last resort, have no appellate jurisdiction over the decisions of federal courts.

What is interesting about this situation is that the common sense expectation that, absent the checking function provided by the fear of reversal, the federal courts play fast and loose with state law in the cases in which they are obliged to adhere to it is wrong. If anything, federal courts may be more scrupulous in fulfilling the obligation of abiding by controlling precedent than they are when federal law controls, although in the latter instance they are at least nominally subject to review by the Supreme Court.

The lesson for the advocate is that the range of permissible argument in these cases is more narrow than it might be in purely federal cases. It is impermissible to urge the overturning of or departure from state authority. Hence, the advocate must seek either to bring her case within existing state doctrine or, at most, demonstrate that other developments in the state's jurisprudence make it unlikely that the state itself would follow its previous ruling. In other words, the federal court of appeals must be addressed in these cases in substantially the same way one would address the intermediate appellate court of the state despite the fact that its decision will not be subject to further review.

Because the Supreme Court hears so few cases, the job of development and exposition even of federal law falls to a great extent on the courts of appeals. Moreover, at least within their own circuits, they speak authoritatively unless reversed by the Supreme Court. Thus, vis-a-vis the district courts in the circuit, the court of appeals is like a court of last resort; although there may be some attempt at intercircuit consistency, the geographic boundaries of a circuit remain very much like the political boundaries of the state.

As a result, it is perhaps not too much to say that more than in other appellate courts the twin functions of correction of error in the particular case and exposition of law to guide decision in other cases are equally significant. Thus, the sort of argument one makes is likely to depend far more on the sort of issue being addressed than on the nature of the tribunal. One can generalize less from the nature of the court than is the case with other tribunals.

There are occasions on which the advocate will know that one or the other function is likely to predominate. Perhaps the clearest instance occurs when the court, either at the urging of counsel or on its own motion, undertakes to hear a case *en banc*. Ordinarily, judges of the courts of appeals sit in panels of three, although there may be more than three judges on a court of appeals. When a case is to be considered *en banc*, all the judges of the court participate in hearing and deciding it. It should be obvious that the decision to sit *en banc* is not one reached lightly. Given the volume of cases to be decided, courts do not go out of their way to have ten judges hear a case that could just as appropriately be heard by three. Consequently, when the court agrees to sit *en banc*, it is not for the purpose of correcting a particular error in a particular case. It is simi-

lar to a court of last resort agreeing to exercise
its discretionary jurisdiction over a case. It is a
clear sign that the court's concerns reach beyond
the particular case and the advocate would be
well-advised to fashion her argument accordingly.

§ 4-4. The United States Supreme Court

At the apex of the judicial hierarchy in the
United States sits the Supreme Court. The experience of appearing before that body is the high
point of many advocates' careers. It is here that
the greatest impact on the *corpus juris* can be
made. This is Olympus. And yet there is no
categorical difference between presenting a case
here and presenting a case before any other court
of last resort. The differences are all differences
of degree or focus. Moreover, anxiety apart, in
some ways the advocate may have an easier time
of it before this body than before less august
courts.

First, to a much greater degree than is true of
many other courts, the bench is a known quanti-
ty. The views, philosophy, methods of thought of
the Justices are revealed in their prior opinions
and widely available. Even with respect to the
particular issues in the case being argued, it is
not unusual to be able to predict which Justices
would resolve the case in favor of one party,
which would find for the other and, most important, which are most open to persuasion. In cas-

es in which this can be predicted with assurance, the advocate may elect to pitch her argument at those "swing" votes. Unfortunately, such predictions are sometimes notoriously wide of the mark. What may be observed with greater accuracy is the sort of approach particular Justices take with respect to certain kinds of issues. There are institutional concerns, for example, to which different Justices react in characteristic ways. A Douglas views the role of the Court vis-a-vis the political branches in one way; a Frankfurter views it in a quite different way. There are a number of overriding political or process concerns common to many of the cases with which the Court deals on which the bent of its members is widely known. It is the foolish advocate who fails to take these concerns into account in planning her presentation.

The views of particular Justices apart, the role of the Court is such that arguments narrowly focused on issues of justice between the parties based on the particular facts revealed by the record are not likely to appeal to those who will decide the case. The Court's institutional role and its own perception of its responsibilities require that the advocate paint on a larger canvas. In our system, the Supreme Court acts as referee in the exercise of power and responsibility among different governmental bodies, state and federal, and between them and the citizen.

That the Court hears and decides relatively few cases means that those few must carry the burden of the policy-making, direction-pointing, law-defining function of the Court. When few cases are heard each one weighs more heavily on the Court's discharge of its responsibility. This can be seen in the criteria the Court has established to determine the cases it will consider each term. (Although nominally the Court has a mandatory as well as a discretionary jurisdiction, the Court's ability to assign cases for summary or plenary treatment operates to render its jurisdiction, in effect, almost entirely discretionary.) Supreme Court Rule 19 declares the considerations governing the Court's exercise of discretion to review. The standards have to do with the importance of the question and the need for guidance of the lower courts.

What all this implies for the advocate is that more than any other judicial body the Supreme Court must be concerned with the operation and effects of its decisions on future cases. Its role of guiding the development of the law through individual decisions with wide impact calls for a style of argument with a markedly different focus than one might employ before tribunals with less far-reaching responsibilities. The advocate must communicate not only the particular problem with which the case is concerned, but the ways in which the case is representative of that problem in a wider context and the necessity for its resolution in the manner for which she is contending. Principle becomes far more significant than precedent. Emphasis on the reason underlying the rule and the operation of both in the real world and on future cases is far more likely to be successful than an argument based on a technical analysis demonstrating the doctrinal impurity of the opinion below.

This is not to say that the advocate before the Supreme Court can safely ignore doctrinal constraints in favor of a free-wheeling policy-based approach. Justices of the Supreme Court, like other judges, value craft and are likely to react negatively to the advocate who ignores the values of craft. Nonetheless, craftsmanship alone is rarely sufficient. One must also show how her position will result in a more sensible accommodation of competing values than that advanced by her adversary. It is this broader concern, requiring the use of a greater range of skills and sophistication, as much as the prestige of the Court, that makes the argument before the Supreme Court as exhilarating a professional experience as the appellate advocate is likely to have.

CHAPTER FIVE

TAXONOMY OF CASES

§ 5–1. The Importance of Classification

The sort of argument an able advocate advances depends to a considerable extent upon the nature of the case to be argued. Cases can be classified in a number of different ways: by doctrinal subject matter—contracts, torts; by source of controlling law—common law, statute, constitution, regulation; by the task to be performed by the court—law application, statutory interpretation, establishment of a new rule of law to govern a case of first impression. No taxonomy is inherently better than any other and the categories of any system are likely to overlap to a considerable extent with others. The appropriate system of classification depends upon the purpose to be served by the act of classifying. Thus, in any given case, several systems of classification may be used for different purposes.

For example, one important taxonomy classifies a case by the kind of task the court must perform in resolving it. Under this system a case may involve a question of the application of a well settled rule of law to the facts of the particular case. It may involve a question of first impression, either in the particular jurisdiction or generally. It may involve an interpretation of the language of a contract, regulation, statute or constitutional provision.

In each kind of case the task of the court, and hence the task of the advocate, differs from what it would be if the case were of a different sort. Consequently, whatever sort of case it is, the advocate ought to let the court know that it is that kind of case. Often the character of the argument is given shape by the category into which the case falls and the argument is more likely to be successful if the court is provided with the appropriate context. For example, if the case calls for the application of an established rule—if the court is not being asked to formulate a new rule of law—it is a good idea to tell that to the court: "This case involves the application of the well established rule that foreseeable damages are recoverable in an action for breach of contract." In such a case it ought to be sufficient to state the rule, citing appropriate authority but to direct the main force of the argument to the facts that bring the case within or place it without the ambit of the rule.

Similarly, if the case involves a question of first impression in the jurisdiction, the court should be so advised. By doing so the advocate establishes why resort is being had to other authority, "Although the question has not been addressed by the courts of this jurisdiction, other courts have considered the question." The shape of the argument in such a case would focus less on the particular facts of the case and more on an analysis and evaluation of the reasoning of the cases in other jurisdictions.

Likewise, if the case is one of first impression not only in this, but also in any other jurisdiction, correspondingly more effort must be expended on basic reasoning. It is important for the advocate not merely to be able to persuade the court to reach a desired conclusion, but also to provide the theory, arguments and authority that will serve as the basis for an opinion likely to be looked to by other courts.

If the interpretation of language is involved, context, purpose, history and other aids to construction will form the backbone of the argument. In any of the foregoing cases, the court will be better able to understand the thrust of the argument if the kind of task to be accomplished is made clear to them at the outset.

A different taxonomy—one perhaps more familiar—reflects the doctrinal subject matter of the cases. This mode of classification may be quite broad or relatively narrow. For example, a case can be classified as civil or criminal or, more narrowly, contract or tort, or homicide or theft. Different doctrinal contexts may suggest different approaches to the cases. Cases also can be classified in accordance with the source of the law to be applied to them: administrative regulation cases, statutory cases, constitutional cases, common law cases. Each requires more or less subtly different approaches from the others. Any particular case is likely to fall within more than one category, of course. A contract case, for example, may well be governed by the statutory provisions of the Uniform Commercial Code.

Of the various categories into which cases can be classified, perhaps none is more significant—at least in terms of frequency of occurrence—than the common law case. Included within this designation are those cases the resolution of which is to be found in (or, perhaps more precisely, the argument of which depends upon) prior judicial pronouncements. Such cases can be distinguished from those governed by the command of statute, constitution, or rule prescribed by some non-judicial body (or some judicial body acting in a non-judicial way: e.g., promulgating rules of procedure not incident to the decision of a dispute). There is, as one might expect, considerable overlap between the common law case and other sorts of cases within this taxonomy. In the statutory case, for example (unless the case is the first to arise under the statute and sometimes even then) the court must consider what prior decisions have done with respect to this or like questions. Similarly, cases whose resolution ultimately depends upon what a constitution or regulation says, must also take into account what other opinions have said they said. Thus, the techniques or approaches appropriate to the common law case are likely also to be useful in arguing other sorts of cases with common law overtones.

Perhaps the most significant doctrinal classification for the advocate is the substance-procedure dichotomy. Procedural issues often require different kinds and styles of argument from those likely to be most effective in a case in which the principal issues concern the formulation or application of substantive legal doctrine. Similarly, civil cases and criminal cases are different in important respects. Contracts cases differ in the approach to be taken to them from torts cases. In the next several sections we shall consider the ways in which the characteristics of cases arising in different doctrinal areas suggest differences in the way one presents them, with special emphasis on their effects in the formulation of argument themes. Following that we shall undertake a similar examination of the various categories of cases classified according to the source of the applicable law.

Because the differences in the way one argues cases in the various categories depends upon the fundamental differences among them, the following sections are necessarily rather abstract. Their purpose is to illuminate, for each category, the underlying values sought to be furthered by the subsystem of doctrine of the particular area. It is only upon such an understanding that the advocate can develop a theme appropriate to her argument. Obviously, more is required to accomplish this than an appreciation of the bases of particular categories; but the appreciation of fundamentals is essential. It is by building on these foundations that the advocate develops an effective presentation. To ignore them is to build a house of cards. Consequently, although the remainder of this chapter may appear somewhat recondite, the theoretical understandings sought to be conveyed are an important part of the advocate's intellectual arsenal.

§ 5–2. Procedure Cases

In arguing cases in which some question of procedure is involved the purpose of procedural rules dictates the thematic approaches likely to be successful. That purpose rarely has much to do with the merits of the underlying controversy between the parties. It is, rather, to move cases efficiently through the judicial system. Thus, the sorts of issues we must consider within this category may variously be denominated procedural, jurisdictional, remedial and those sorts of questions of equity practice having to do with such things as, for example, the adequacy of legal remedies or whether the prerequisites for injunctive relief have been established.

The sorts of questions with which we are here concerned may arise either as a collateral issue in the case or may present the central issue to be decided. There are important differences in the way the effective advocate handles these two situations. In cases in which the procedural issue is collateral it is often important to emphasize the underlying issues as a context in which the procedural problem arises. As a practical matter it may be easier to persuade the court to overlook procedural niceties that would bar a decision on the merits if the merits are especially compelling. On the other hand, if the advocate can persuade the court either that the underlying question is a difficult one or that it is one having far-reaching consequences, the full effect of which may not yet be apparent, a procedural device permitting the court to avoid deciding the merits may be welcomed. In short, in cases in which both procedural and substantive issues are presented, the effective advocate may play one off against the other.

Perhaps the best known example is Chief Justice Marshall's political manipulation of procedural and substantive issues in *Marbury v. Madison*, 5 U.S. (1 Cranch) 137 (1803). The substantive issue (Marbury's right to his commission) had to be decided in favor of Marbury if the new nation's delicate system of checks and balances was to emerge from this confrontation unscathed; but, for the same reasons, a head-on clash between the judiciary and the executive had to be avoided. Marshall's "backwards" opinion is still considered a brilliant, if unprincipled, solution. By taking up the procedural issue (whether mandamus could issue from the Supreme Court) after the substantive issues had been resolved, Marshall was able to render the legally necessary opinion without precipitating a crisis. Had he proceeded in the jurisprudentially correct order by treating the procedural problems as a threshold issue, he would not have been able to reach the matter of the commission, because an opinion in that framework would have been purely advisory. (Of course, it was, in effect, no more than that when rendered.)

By contrast, in cases in which the procedural question is the central issue in the case, such a playing-off is not likely to be successful. In such cases the values at stake are fairness and efficiency in the broad sense—including such notions as the role of the court vis-a-vis other institutions of government whether it is the most "efficient" decisionmaker, as well as those sometimes more narrow mechanisms within the judicial system that govern the adjudicatory process. In some cases these values are pitted against each other. In others the battle is fought over which side will promote fairness. Finally, the controversy may focus upon which result will lead to greater efficiency.

Typically, but not ineluctably, the fairness versus efficiency argument can also be framed in terms of doing justice between the parties contrasted with preserving systemic values. The argument in such a case will seem quite similar to that in which procedural and substantive issues are intertwined. So, for example, where the question is one of jurisdiction, the absence of another forum to redress the claimed wrong must be considered and weighed against the institutional costs of extending jurisdiction. Typical are some of the standing, ripeness and mootness cases. It was just such an argument that carried the day in the abortion cases before the Supreme Court. The Court noted that the normal delays in litigation would, under a strict analysis, render any abortion case moot before it could reach the Supreme Court. Characterizing the issue as one "capable of repetition yet evading review," the Court refused to allow the procedural impediment to prevent it from reaching the merits. *Roe v. Wade*, 410 U.S. 113, 124–25, 93 S.Ct. 705, 713 (1973). The Court could just as easily have avoided deciding on the merits of a difficult case by finding a procedural barrier. It has done so in the past. In *Tileston v. Ullman*, 318 U.S. 44, 63 S.Ct. 493 (1943), for example, the plaintiff-physician's lack of standing to raise the issue was used to avoid the necessity of addressing the question of the right of married adults to use contraceptives.

Another, somewhat different, manifestation of the balancing of interests may be seen in many equity suits in which a request for equitable relief must address the adequacy of legal remedies in light of the particular injury alleged. Nuisance cases are but one example. Typically, the plaintiff will argue that the only adequate relief is injunctive: close down the drive-in; ban late-night arrivals and departures from the airport; force the factory to clean up its wastes. The defendant will counter that money damages representing any diminution in the value of plaintiff's property are sufficient, especially in view of the social worth of the offending enterprise and the burden injunctive relief would impose on it.

In procedural cases in which both sides claim to further the fairness values, the best arguments are those through which it can be demonstrated that fairness and systemic efficiency run hand-in-hand. Typical are some of the cases in which trial counsel has failed to make a record adequate to preserve a particular error by neglecting to object to some action or ruling of the trial judge or by otherwise failing to make a proper record. The argument in favor of adhering strictly to procedural requirements will stress the unfairness of providing repeated opportunities to one party to which the other must repeatedly respond—the two bites of the apple argument. The other side will stress the technical nature of procedural rules and urge that they ought not stand in the way of doing substantial justice. The liberalization of the once highly technical rules of pleading exemplifies this viewpoint. Pleadings today are liberally construed and may be amended with much greater freedom than had been true in earlier times.

Similarly, in cases in which a procedural rule operates as a time bar, one party will urge the justice of a policy of repose; the other will press the injustice of allowing the mere passage of time to bar an otherwise meritorious claim. It was just such arguments which led most states to change their limitations law for malpractice suits. At one time virtually all states held that the statute of limitations began running at the time the injury occurred (the day the doctor left the sponge in or the day the attorney, after imperfectly searching the title, reported it marketable to his client). Attorneys for victims who did not become aware of the problem until perhaps years later argued fairness (the unsophisticated plaintiff cannot be expected to know there's a sponge in his stomach or a lien on his title until it gives him trouble—that's why he hired a professional in the first place); attorneys for the professionals urged support for the policy of repose. (The compromise adopted almost universally is the obvious one: limitations begin running when the injured person discovers, or should have discovered, the professional's error.) Similar arguments, arguments in which the question turns on the justice of a policy of repose and finality, may be found in cases raising issues of collateral estoppel or res judicata.

Finally, there are those cases in which both sides claim the values of efficiency. Typical are the cases in which one side seeks interlocutory review of a trial court's order while the other side opposes such review—cases in which the issue is the application of the final judgment rule, so-called. That rule (much simplified for our purposes) requires that review of any errors alleged to have occurred at trial must await the entry of a final judgment. The efficiency objective is obvious: Immediate review of alleged errors could require repeated interruptions of the proceedings while appeals were taken, as well as repetitive engagements of the appeal mechanism with all of the collateral requirements that that would entail. Moreover, the outcome of the trial might be in favor of the party who seeks early review of these claimed errors making interlocutory review unnecessary.

Far better, as a general rule, to await the conclusion of the trial process. At that point some errors may have been rendered irrelevant by a desired judgment, relieving the appellate court of the necessity of dealing with them. Even where that has not occurred, the effect of any particular error is likely to be easier to evaluate in the context of the entire proceeding; finally, the appellate court is able to deal with all claims of error during a single proceeding.

Yet, there are cases in which it can be argued that application of the final judgment rule is inefficient. For example, in cases in which a reversal of a particular ruling made early in the proceeding would obviate the necessity for further proceedings it would be most efficient to secure that reversal early in the game. This is the basis of 28 U.S.C.A. § 1292(b), authorizing interlocutory appeals when the trial judge certifies that the order appealed from "involves a controlling question of law as to which there is substantial ground for difference of opinion and that an immediate appeal from the order may materially advance the ultimate termination of the litigation . . . ." The difficulty, of course, is that this is true only to the extent that review results in reversal; and that cannot be known until after review has been granted.

Nonetheless, there are recognized exceptions to the final judgment rule. As with most exceptions to most rules, these rest on the notion that the objectives and bases of the rule do not exist on the particular facts. For example, if one of the reasons for the rule is that the effects of any particular error can be more accurately ascertained in the context of the entire proceeding, where this is not so—where the ruling for which review is sought is collateral to the case—there is less force to the argument favoring application of the rule. Thus, the Supreme Court has held the denial of a motion requiring plaintiff to post security for defendant's costs was an appealable order, although no final judgment on the merits had yet been rendered, because the particular claim was both important and separable from the merits. *Cohen v. Beneficial Industrial Loan Corp.*, 337 U. S. 541, 69 S.Ct. 1221 (1949).

It should be obvious that the categories we have been discussing—arguments based on fairness, arguments based on efficiency—are hardly water-tight compartments. Most arguments based on efficiency have overtones of fairness values; most fairness arguments cannot ignore the needs of systemic efficiency. Indeed, the most persuasive arguments are those which demonstrate that fairness values will be furthered with little sacrifice to efficiency values, or that efficiency values will be furthered with no sacrifice to fairness or, best of all, that both fairness and efficiency counsel a favorable ruling.

One other insight should be noted with respect to those arguments in which both sides rely upon the same value, whether it be efficiency or fairness. As with most arguments in which the central issue is which position will further an agreed upon value, one of the parties will focus on the particular while the other addresses the general. Thus, if the single dimension argument is based on fairness, one side will argue the fairness of a particular *result*; the others will argue the fairness of the *rule*. Similarly, if both parties claim to represent the value of efficiency, one side will argue the efficiency of a particular result while the other argues the efficiency of a particular rule.

This phenomenon can be illustrated by the effect of procedural rules concerning counterclaims. The federal rules focus on efficiency: any counterclaim arising out of the same transaction must be asserted by the defendant when he is sued or it is foregone. State rules, on the other hand, may treat such counterclaims as permissive in the interest of fairness; for example, the defendant may prefer a separate trial on his claim or, if sued in federal court, a local forum.

Assume that A, a mason in Idaho Falls, is hired to do the block and brick work on a construction project in Jackson, Wyoming, for which B is the general contractor. While working on the site, A is injured because of the negligence of B's employees and files suit in federal court.

After the building is completed and occupied, but before A's action against B is ready for trial, defects in construction due to A's negligence become apparent. B, however, does not counterclaim against A; rather, he files a separate suit against A in state court in Wyoming. A successfully moves for dismissal, based on B's "default" or "waiver" in federal court.

On appeal, B's attorney will be likely to argue fairness of result: her client should not be forced into a particular forum; the state court is the more appropriate and better qualified tribunal to hear the case; the plaintiff is entitled to a local jury; and, although the same transaction did give rise to both claims, the issues are totally different and trying them together would prejudice her client.

A's attorney can also argue fairness, but of the rule: it enables both parties to make better tactical decisions because they can act without worrying about subsequent suits; it keeps inconvenience to the parties to a minimum; it enables the jury to reach a decision based on all relevant information; and, even if the rule's fairness is not apparent here, its operation does not prejudice either party and an exception, if permitted, would open the door to other, less appropriate exceptions.

§ 5–3. Criminal Appeals

The criminal case presents what may be the most dramatic conflict of values of any within the adjudicatory system. The values of law and order, of public safety, of the integrity of society are pitted against the values of individual liberty, strict standards of fairness and the integrity of the legal system. The importance of the values on both sides of the scale distinguish the criminal case—and hence, the criminal appeal—from other kinds of cases within the system. Thus, for our purposes the category, "the criminal appeal" encompasses all cases in which the representatives of society are pitted against one who is alleged to have breached its standards and from whom some penalty is sought to be exacted. While the category, therefore, encompasses more than appeals from convictions (it includes, as well, for example, collateral attacks on convictions and appeals brought by the state from dismissals of indictments) defendants' challenges to their convictions are surely the most common form in which criminal appeals arise.

Because all criminal appeals involve the same collision of values (at least at this level of abstraction), it is possible to discern recurring themes that pervade the cases. These themes are of three kinds and virtually any criminal case can be argued with reference to one of them. The first has to do with the integrity of the factfinding function of the trial; the second with the violation of rights and resultant injury—to the accused by the state, or to the victim and the state by the accused; the third involves systemic problems of the criminal justice system, including, for example, questions of prosecutorial or judicial discretion, questions of finality or, in some collateral attack cases, the relationship between federal and state court systems.

(Other sorts of problems may arise, of course, in the criminal justice process; but they are not peculiar to that process and are therefore more effectively treated as belonging to a different taxonomy. For example, it is not uncommon for questions to arise concerning the elements of a particular offense with which the defendant was charged. Such a question does not appear to fall within one of the three categories described above. It is the sort of question, however, not at all peculiar to the criminal process *qua* criminal process and its more appropriately dealt with as a statutory case or a case requiring the same sort of analysis as any common law civil action in which the analytic elements of the claim or defense are in dispute. Similarly, a claim that a particular activity is beyond the power of the state to prohibit presents issues and values more closely related to the constitutional case than to the criminal case and hence is more effectively treated as belonging to the former class.)

Among the major purposes of the criminal trial (indeed, of all trials) is determining historical truth—the accurate recounting of what happened. Because the stakes are so high—liberty—society places very great importance on this function. That is why, for example, the burden of persuasion the prosecution must meet before the defendant may be convicted is proof beyond a reasonable doubt. Thus, any claim of error that may have affected the accuracy of the findings of fact at trial requires careful scrutiny. Society needs to feel quite certain that an innocent person has not been convicted. The typical claim of error raising this kind of issue is one challenging the admission or exclusion of evidence—restrictions on cross-examination, admission of other crimes evidence or other evidentiary rulings that may have led the fact-finder to a conclusion different from that which would have been reached had the evidentiary ruling been otherwise. That last qualification is crucial in this sort of case. The claim is not merely that some error was committed, but that that error infected the integrity of the fact-finding process—that in the absence of that error the result would have, or at least might have, been different.

Such will be the axis upon which the defendant's argument will turn. This argument can be narrowed in several ways which perhaps can be better illustrated by examining the sorts of themes likely to form the centerpiece of the prosecution's argument for upholding the ruling of the trial court. Assume, for example, that the defendant had taken the witness stand and that the trial court had permitted the prosecution to impeach her by introducing evidence of the defendant's prior criminal record. The defendant would argue that this evidence did not affect her credibility as a witness and prejudiced the jury against her.

First, the prosecution may argue that the claimed error was, in fact, not error, but a correct application of legal principles because as a general matter the rule applied below either does not affect the validity of fact-finding or it enhances it. That is, the prosecution would argue that prior criminal activity does affect credibility and should be considered by the jury in order to enable it to assess the veracity of the witness.

Second, the prosecution may argue that quite apart from the general principle, its application in the particular case enhanced the validity of fact-finding or did not affect it. That is, even if there is a general rule prohibiting impeachment of a defendant-witness by introducing evidence of prior convictions, the prosecution might argue that the particular prior conviction was for perjury, thus having a direct bearing on credibility, while the charge for which the defendant is now being prosecuted is assault so that the prior dissimilar perjury conviction would not be prejudicial. If the prosecution's theory is that the *particular* ruling enhanced fact-finding, she will be arguing for an exception to the general rule or a recasting of it that would permit or require the action which formed the ground of appeal or, in extreme cases, for a decision that the rule is wrong or obsolete and should be abolished. Thus, the prosecutor might contend that a rule prohibiting impeachment of a defendant by introducing previous convictions is limited to those convictions not relevant to veracity or that, in general, a defendant ought to be impeachable by prior convictions. If the prosecution's argument is that the ruling below had no effect on the verdict, neither beneficial nor harmful, her argument will be based on the notion of harmless error. What ought to be noted is that each of these thematic responses accepts the notion of the integrity of the fact-finding function of the trial as the axis upon which the appeal should revolve.

The prosecutor may, of course, attempt to switch the argument to entirely new ground. She may stress, for example, the needs of public safety, the heinousness of the offense, the evil nature of the defendant. Of course, she must also

respond to her adversary's argument based upon
the accuracy of the trial result; but by stressing
these other matters, by using them as the thematic base upon which her argument is built, she
may be able to minimize the accuracy problem.
If successful, this approach increases at least
the rhetorical burden upon the defendant-appel-
lant. This argument is especially useful when
combined with the harmless error argument, for
it subtly and subliminally changes the quality of
that argument from "any error committed did
not affect the verdict" to "any error committed
should not affect the verdict." It is the legal
equivalent of the lay view that a criminal ought
not get off on a technicality. And because
judges, too, are members of society with many of
the same values and fears of other citizens, the
appeal of the argument, when put into institutionally acceptable form, is obvious.

The defendant may also use a variation of this
theme. Instead of challenging the accuracy of
the verdict, the defendant may argue the need to
restrain government overreaching, in order to
safeguard the rights of citizens from abuse by
public authority. One is apt to see this sort of
argument in cases in which there is little reason
to doubt the accuracy of the verdict. It seeks to
establish the proposition that the particular result is less important than the means used to
achieve it. Perhaps the best example of this sort

of thematic approach can be seen in appeals seeking to overturn convictions procured through illegally seized evidence. It is, of course, plain that the means by which evidence is secured does not affect its probative value. Thus, the integrity of the fact-finding process remains unimpaired. Indeed, suppressing such evidence necessarily reduces the accuracy of the verdict. Nonetheless, the judgment has been made that the protection of the values of personal privacy and security from the abuse of governmental power is of greater importance.

Finally, there are the arguments based on themes of systemic or institutional values. These are often closely related to the procedural arguments considered in the last section. What is distinctive about this type of argument is that it rarely concerns itself with the immediate parties or the concrete merits of the particular case. So, for example, the failure to make an appropriate objection at trial may preclude relief on appeal regardless of the merits of the underlying issue because the values of procedural regularity require such a result. (Interestingly, there are escape devices from results based upon these values if the results are otherwise intolerable. For example, the notion of plain error, discussed more fully in Section 2–3 permits the appellate court to ignore a failure to preserve a point for appeal if the error complained of is sufficiently egregious.)

§ 5–4. Contract Cases

There are three kinds of contract cases with which we need to be concerned. The first raises issues relating to the content of the agreement; that is, questions about what the parties agreed to do or to refrain from doing—the rights and obligations assumed by the parties to the transaction. The second set of cases, by contrast, presents issues of validity. Assuming we know to what the parties agreed, should that agreement be given legal effect? The third category of issues that may arise in contract litigation concerns the appropriate division of loss resulting from a failure of one of the parties to perform the obligations of the agreement. This category includes such topics as the appropriate measure of damages or availability of other remedies, mitigation, impossibility of performance, excuse and so forth. We shall deal with these three distinct sorts of issues in turn. It should be noted, however, as we have pointed out earlier, that our categories are not water-tight. The same case may raise issues of interpretation as well as issues of validity, or loss distribution. Cases in which the question is the presence or absence of consideration sufficient to support an agreement, for example, typically involve issues both of interpretation and validity. And, of course, in such cases, it is generally a mistake to treat the issues as entirely distinct. By far the better argument is one in which each issue is permitted to feed off the others symbiotically.

Contract cases of the first type can be profitably compared with statutory cases. They are alike in that both typically require that content be given language intended to have operative legal significance. They differ in that private parties entering into private arrangements are likely to be operating in narrower, more various and more specialized contexts than are public bodies seeking to achieve public ends. As in statutory cases—as in any kind of case in which it is necessary to interpret language—a two-tiered analysis can be useful. First, the advocate may argue for a particular theory of interpretation: plain language, intent of the draftsmen, purpose to be served and so forth. Second the advocate may argue for a particular meaning to be given the relevant language.

Thus, it is useful to distinguish contract cases from other kinds of cases through the notion of private legislation. Two (or more) private parties come together and agree on the rules that are to govern a particular facet of their relationship and then further agree on the language reflecting that agreement. Because private relationships and the contexts in which they occur are so varied and specialized, however, the task of determining what the parties sought to accomplish by their agreement may be an extraordinarily difficult one. The same words can have quite different meanings in an agreement between professional engineers and one between shopkeepers, much less consumers with no specialized knowledge or information.

Consequently, it becomes the job of the advocate to illuminate the context in which the particular agreement in suit was forged. Sound decision of such cases comports with what Karl Llewellyn called "situation sense"; but before that can be achieved one must have a sense of the situation. The court must be educated, therefore, with respect to the commercial and economic realities governing the transaction. Typically, the party that can persuade the court that her version of this reality is the sounder one is likely to prevail. The Uniform Commercial Code, for example, recognizes that agreements between "merchants" (those having special knowledge or skill with respect to the subject matter of an agreement) are not always to be governed by the rules applicable to other agreements. Thus, the Code directs attention to usage of trade to assist in questions of interpretation, *see, e.g.*, U.C.C. § 1–205. Similarly, the remedies available and most appropriate in contract disputes are more likely to be argued about successfully if the argument is directed at the situation in which the dispute arose than if narrowly limited to legal doctrine and precedent.

This kind of argument is critical for another reason as well. In statutory interpretation cases there will often be prior decisions in the same or even other jurisdictions considering similar statutory provisions. These decisions can be looked to, at least for guidance, in interpreting the particular statute whose meaning is in issue. Often similar contexts will have prompted similar legislative responses. Because each contract has its own context, however, decisions interpreting similar language in other agreements may be far less helpful in determining the meaning of this agreement. At the very least, it becomes crucial to demonstrate a similarity of context in the use of particular contractual language. This is reflected in the Uniform Commercial Code's use of "course of dealing" and "usage of trade" as interpretive devices. U.C.C. § 1–205.

The aim of the advocate in this first kind of contract case is to give a sensible meaning to particular language. In the second type of case, in which the primary issue has to do with validity or enforceability, the values sought to be protected are themselves in conflict. On one side are the arguments based on notions of personal autonomy and freedom of contract; on the other are the arguments based upon fairness and the equalization of advantage. To say that at bottom these values form the theme of the arguments for or against contract validity is, perhaps, to say the obvious, for these are the values and the tension that underlie much of the law of contract. Yet, although it is critical that the advocate be considerably more artful in her presentation than merely to assert these abstract values, it is equally important that she recognize that, however the more concrete theme of the argument is formulated, it is upon these values that it must ultimately rest. The unconscionability and duress cases familiar to all first year contracts students are typical of this classification. *See, e.g., Williams v. Walker-Thomas Furniture Co.*, 350 F.2d 445 (D.D.C.Cir. 1965); *S. P. Dunham & Co. v. Kudra*, 44 N.J.Super. 565, 131 A.2d 306 (1957).

The final category of contract cases involves questions of the appropriate apportionment of the losses resulting from a deal gone sour. Often the arguments in such cases will overlap with arguments based upon the meaning to be given the agreement. The advocates may argue that the division of losses was or was not considered and incorporated within the contract and should or should not be given effect. The factors we have already considered with respect to questions of validity and interpretation would also apply in this third type of case.

Sometimes, however, it is clear that the parties have not considered loss distribution. In cases in which that situation obtains, the advocates' arguments are likely to turn upon the values of fairness and efficiency. As in the cases in which the meaning of the contract is in dispute, determining the appropriate remedy for breach requires that the court be educated concerning the context of the parties and the agreement in the world of economics and commerce. It is up to the advocates to supply this education. Such elements as the ability to avoid the loss through the contract or by collateral agreements with third parties, power to minimize the injury, or, at least, to spread it—in short, questions about the economic sense of imposing the risk of loss on one party rather than another—are likely to be the focus of this sort of case.

§ 5–5. Tort Cases

As with all other kinds of cases within the doctrinal taxonomy, effective underlying themes of arguments in tort cases reflect the values with which that area of law is concerned. The major concerns of which the advocate must be aware are three: the compensation value, the deterrence value and the efficiency value. Again, as has been true in other areas, the values often overlap with particular cases implicating one or more of them. Also as has been true in other areas, the most effective argument is likely to be one that is consistent with all three values. Finally, and again as has been true in other areas, a particular case may involve predominantly either intravalue argument or intervalue argument. That is to say, each advocate may argue that her position will result in a more equitable distribution of loss or will affect primary behavior in a particular and beneficial way (intravalue); or one advocate may argue that compensation is the more important value to be furthered in the case and that her position advances that value while the other advocate argues that efficiency is the more important value in the particular case and that her position advances that value (intervalue).

To the extent that the compensation value is the dimension in which the arguments are advanced, plaintiff will be likely to emphasize her injury, the fault of the defendant and the superior financial resources of the defendant (either independently or through insurance or other cost spreading techniques). The defendant will seek to minimize its blameworthiness, minimize the plaintiff's injury and suggest the plaintiff's own blameworthiness. In short, the compensation argument is often presented in rather stark white hat versus black hat terms. It is the young mother who has been run down by the corporate limousine. It is this which, if carefully done, makes it so effective. It is also its greatest danger. For if overdone it is likely to result in resentment from the bench. It is far too easy to fall into the trap of emotionalism—to argue to the appellate bench as one might argue to a trial jury. It is almost always a mistake. In this sort of argument understatement is especially important. The impression the advocate seeks to create should be conveyed through very careful word choice with the emotional impact of the events giving rise to the suit providing at most only a strong undercurrent to the argument.

The argument based upon the deterrence value is one manifestation of the policy-centered argument described in some detail in Section 6–4. It is a theme that relies upon persuading the court that a particular rule will have a particular effect upon primary behavior. Thus, the advocates may agree upon the behavioral ends to be achieved; if so, the argument will be framed in terms of which rule is more likely to achieve those ends; or the advocates may disagree about the behavioral ends themselves. For instance, any time punitive damages are awarded, the court is attempting to deter future harmful behavior; such damages are also called "exemplary" because their purpose is to set an example for others, rather than to compensate the injured party. If punitives are at issue, the advocate seeking them usually has some powerful social policy arguments available to her.

The different standards applied by courts in defamation cases reflect this focus on behavioral objectives. Punitive damages may be awarded in some defamation actions, suggesting that courts wish to deter future libels; but the standard under which they will be awarded is a difficult one to meet, because the courts also wish to protect —encourage, even—freedom of speech.   When the plaintiff is a public figure, even the standard of liability is based on "actual malice," because the behavioral goal of disseminating information of public interest is more important than protecting the individual reputations of celebrities.   In such a case, the advocates' arguments are virtually outlined for them in advance.

Finally, there is the argument whose theme is the value of social or economic efficiency.   Unlike the sort of efficiency with which we were concerned in the procedural case, efficiency in the management of litigation, the focus here is on efficiency in the world beyond the courtroom. Does it make good economic or social sense that a particular risk be insured against?   Which party is in a better position to insure?   Ought the inevitability of loss be shared by an entire industry as one of the costs of doing business—enterprise liability—or is it better simply to let the loss lie where it falls?   There is a strong flavor of social engineering attached to the efficiency argument.

Thus, torts cases present perhaps the most challenging category of litigation about which to generalize with respect to thematic approaches. The area of human conduct for which one must consult the law of torts is more varied than in most other fields with which we have been concerned and the principles underlying the law governing that conduct must, as a consequence, be more responsive to a greater and more varied number of values. At the very least, a rather sophisticated process of refinement, of narrowing and polishing the theme upon which the advocate relies, is necessary to reflect the more concrete manifestations of these rather abstract themes.

§ 5–6. The Administrative Case

Not every case coming to an appellate court from an administrative agency is an administrative case as the term is used here. Those cases, for example, in which the jurisdiction of the agency to hear the dispute is at issue have far more in common with the statutory case considered in the next section than with the more frequent review of agency decisionmaking which concerns us in this section. (The jurisdiction of an administrative agency is, of course, determined by statute.) Our focus in this section is more narrowly limited to challenges to the result reached by an administrative agency in the particular case before the court.

If the typical constitutional case (see Section 5–8) is at one end of a continuum, the typical administrative case is likely to be at the other end. The far-ranging value-laden decision-making process often found in constitutional adjudication is rarely present in reviews of agency decisions. Here, for obvious reasons, the focus is considerably narrower.

This narrow focus has significant implications for the style of argument likely to be successful in such cases. For example, a successful argument challenging an agency's determination is likely to be fact-specific. The argument supporting the agency will almost certainly rely heavily on the presumption favoring the agency based upon its experience and expertise. Although rarely articulated, the strength of this presumption, as a practical matter, varies considerably in accordance with two factors: the court's evaluation of the particular agency at the time and the sort of problem the agency is charged with handling. As might be expected, the more familiar the subject matter of the proceeding is to the general experience of the court, *i.e.*, the easier it is for the court to comprehend what is going on, the more likely is it that the court will exercise an independent judgment rather than relying on agency expertise. Thus, a court may react quite differently in a case challenging an agency determination in a civil rights case involving racial discrimination in employment from the way it might react in a case challenging an agency's determination in an air pollution case involving the appropriate methods of measuring various kinds of pollutants and the propriety of employing competing remedial technological devices to reduce them. Because of the factual and theoretical complexity of the issues in the latter kind of case, a court is far more likely to rely on the expertise of the agency—to limit its review of the agency's decision to determining if the agency's choices among varying scientific or technological theories or proofs are reasonable ones.

Consequently, the key task of the successful advocate in such cases is to explain the record, especially those things in the record difficult for the novice to comprehend, in terms that will allow the court to understand what the agency did and the reasons for its actions. Technical material must be put in lay terms, which means, first of all, that the advocate herself must learn and understand the technical, scientific or specialized body of knowledge in order to be able to communicate it to the court. The bench is either familiar with the law governing the case or at least comfortable with its ability to discover what it must know about the law; it is likely to be far less comfortable with specialized empirical information and the implications and conclusions to be drawn from it.

The advocate must know the record: appreciate the facts, theories and arguments on which the agency based its conclusions and—what is crucial—rehearse the logical route from the evidence in the record to the agency's conclusions in a way comprehensible to a layman. The record should be indexed for the convenience of the court and the specific bits of evidence supporting or weakening particular conclusions should be designated. (The advent of computers and their application to the practice of law should make this formerly onerous and time-consuming task far less formidable.) The idea ought to be to pinpoint each piece of evidence in the record in support of one's position, and to pile one bit of evidence on top of another on top of another on top of another until an unassailable wall of evidence has been erected.

§ 5–7. Statutory Cases

As used here a statutory case is one whose outcome depends upon the interpretation or construction given a formal enactment in specific language adopted by a body charged with the responsibility and authority for its promulgation and having the force of law—constitutions excepted. Thus, included in the term statute are municipal ordinances, federal statutory law, state statutory law, regulations and so forth. What distinguishes the statutory case from other kinds of cases is the necessity for addressing specific language having operative legal significance.

(Contracts cases and constitutional law cases, of course, generally meet this definition and much that is applicable to the statutory case also applies to them. The constitutional case will be considered in the next section. The contract case, considered in some detail in Section 5–4, differs primarily in that the meaning to be imputed to the operative language will have no direct effect on other cases, while the meaning assigned to the language of a statute will continue to be directly effective in other cases arising under the statute unless the decision is overruled or reversed by a higher court.)

In one sense the statutory case is more confining for the advocate than other kinds of cases for the obvious reason that the language of the statute restricts the range of argument available. In another sense, however, the statutory case often permits a wider-ranging argument. For in addition to arguing what the outcome of the case should be, the advocate may also urge a particular *method* of decision on the court. That is, one may argue not only what the statute says but also how to go about the process of determining what the statute says. The case whose outcome depends upon the construction or interpretation of legislation often requires the advocate to articulate not only a theory of the case but also a theory of interpretation. Ideally, of course, one might argue that under any theory of interpretation the statute requires a favorable result.

This is not to say that this two-tiered argument will always be explicit. Sometimes, rather than arguing explicitly for a particular theory of interpretation, the advocate may assume particular theories and seek to establish meaning based on those theories. For example, the advocate may not argue that the court should interpret the language of the statute according to its plain meaning and then, as a separate step argue what that meaning is. Rather, these analytically separate steps may be combined into an argument that says, "The plain meaning of the statute requires (or forbids) . . . " What is important is that in developing her argument the advocate attend the various interpretive approaches available to her in seeking to persuade the court that a statute requires a result for which she contends or forbids a result for which her adversary contends.

There are a number of interpretive arguments upon which the advocate may rely to establish a favorable meaning to a statute. Although a full treatment of the process of statutory interpretation is beyond the scope of this *Nutshell*, the basic approaches to dealing with legislative materials must be considered for they are part of the advocate's stock in trade. The reader should be alerted, however, that we shall be painting with a rather broad brush. A more complete treatment

[*111*]

of the subject can be found in W. Reynolds, *Judicial Process in a Nutshell* 192–286 (1980).

First, and perhaps most obvious, is the argument that relies predominantly on the bare words of the statute. This argument actually consists of two separate steps, although the first is largely intuitive and in practice they are often combined. The first step is to establish that the words of the statute are reasonably clear; the second is to show that they mean what the advocate claims them to mean. What distinguishes this approach from others is that it does not require looking beyond the words of the section of the statute immediately applicable to the case to determine meaning, although there is generally reliance on other sources to confirm the meaning so determined.

The answering argument is likely to be that the statutory language does not bear the meaning claimed for it or that the language alone is not sufficient to establish that meaning. Thus, an additional approach to arguing the statutory case is one that looks beyond the language of the enactment. Once that step is taken, there are a number of sources to which the advocate may resort to illuminate the meaning of the legislation.

Often the particular statutory language or language substantially similar to it in another statute will already have been interpreted. The question then becomes the extent to which the court should apply that earlier interpretation in the case now before it. One might argue, for example, that the administrative agency charged with administering the statutory scheme has interpreted the language consistently in a certain way and that the agency's interpretation should be accorded respect. Likewise, one might argue that similar language in another statute has been interpreted in a particular way by this or some other court and that the language as used in the statute now to be interpreted should be given the same construction. One might respond to such an approach either by urging that the previous interpretation was incorrect or, and likely to be more effective, by demonstrating the differences between the two statutes that render application of the previous interpretation inappropriate. It should be noted, of course, that the style of argument is not significantly different from the way one would ordinarily deal with common law doctrines embodied in prior decisions (See Section 6–3).

A variation of this argument sometimes applicable is that the enacting authority "incorporated" prior judicial constructions of similar language into the present statute. Obviously this would require that the judicial gloss had been added before enactment of the statute now before the court. It is most effective when the particular language in the same statute, now encrusted with judicially imposed meaning, has been reenacted as part of a recodification, amendment or general statutory overhaul.

This approach seeks to determine the legislative will from materials in addition to the statute itself. Thus, resort to legislative history in the form of hearings, reports, speeches and so forth might be used to bolster an argument for a particular meaning. It is the rare case in which the advocate should rely too heavily primarily on legislative history, however. Although as additional support for an interpretation that can be otherwise justified such material may be useful, courts are aware of the extent to which legislative history may be misused or used selectively and, as a result often view it with an appropriately wary eye. Where legislative history is used to support a particular interpretation of statutory language, the advocate should be aware of the different weight likely to be accorded various kinds of legislative history. The isolated remarks of particular legislators are not likely to carry great weight. Committee reports, on the other hand, may be quite influential. Finally, although rarely given explicit recognition, legislative history may be more persuasive in interpreting some statutes than it is in others. In general, the more technical the statute, the more likely is legislative history to play a role in its interpretation.

Sometimes, the particular provision to be interpreted is but one piece of a larger statutory scheme. Where that is so the structure of the statute or the context it provides may be of substantial assistance in arguing for a particular meaning. The more detailed and comprehensive the statutory scheme, for example, the easier it should be to argue against any additions, in the form of remedies or claims not given explicit recognition, through judicial implication.

Regardless of which of these approaches the advocate elects to pursue, they should be used in conjunction with an appeal to the purpose of the statute. It is this notion of statutory purpose that generally will provide the clearest and most convincing focus in arguing the statutory case. The context of the legislation in terms of the social, economic or other problem it was designed to ameliorate is of special importance in persuading a court of the meaning or application of the statutory language. Thus, it is much like the way one uses "situation sense" in the contract case (Section 5–4) although, obviously, one is painting on a substantially larger canvas. In short, the advocate should attempt to demonstrate the problem the statute addresses and the way in which it attempts to solve it. Even this is often not sufficient, however. Greater persuasiveness can be achieved by demonstrating the wisdom of the legislative scheme. Thus, the most persuasive approach is two-pronged: first, the legislature has addressed a particular problem in a particular way; and second, even apart from the legislation, as a matter of sound social policy it is the way the problem ought to be addressed.

Because of the relationship of legislature to court, the latter is not free to disregard the legislative expression of public policy (on other than constitutional grounds). Consequently the advocate must argue not merely what is good policy but what the legislature believed to be good policy. Inherent in every statutory case is some notion of the role of the court within the concept of separation of powers—that courts, absent exceptional circumstances, defer to the wisdom of legislative bodies.

Even more important to the advocate than the formal theoretical proposition that legislatures make law while courts merely "interpret" it, is that most judges—the advocate's audience—believe in this notion of legislative supremacy. It is important for the advocate, therefore, to demonstrate not merely that her position is the better one, but also that her position is the one most consistent with the legislative will. At the same time it is important that the advocate attempt to persuade the court of the wisdom of the legislation—not only that they must follow the legislative directive but that they should.

§ 5–8. Constitutional Cases

As the Supreme Court is to other courts so is the constitutional case to other cases. It is at the zenith of the craft of appellate advocacy, especially if the argument is before a court of last resort (the Supreme Court of the United States for federal constitutional cases, the highest state court for state constitutional cases), but even if it takes place before a tribunal of lesser authority. It is in arguing the constitutional case that the full panoply of the advocate's skills are brought into play. For in addition to representing the most powerful source of positive law in our society, constitutional adjudication has elements of most of the other kinds of cases with which advocates and judges must deal.

Like the statutory case, analysis must begin with exegesis of the text. Regardless of the flexibility that some of the broad abstractions contained in the Constitution permit, it remains a written constitution with the inherent restraints that that imposes. Much of the law of the Constitution, of course, is to be found in the judicial opinions that give meaning to the language of the document. Thus, there is more than a bit of the elements of common law adjudication to be found in constitutional cases, as well. As we shall explore in greater detail below, there are even elements of the administrative case to be found in the constitutional case in the deference to be paid other governmental institutions, state or federal, whose view of the Constitution or whose powers under it are brought into question. Finally, because much constitutional language is open-textured and because *stare decisis* plays a somewhat lesser role in constitutional adjudication, the advocate must be prepared to justify a particular position on grounds of sound public policy.

A Constitution, whether state or federal, provides the basic charter of the government it establishes. It is that document which parcels out power and responsibility, and the limits on both, on the constituent elements of the government; it defines the relationship of the members of society to the state. Thus, constitutional cases are likely to present the fundamental questions of government and society. It is in the consideration of these cases that the courts serve as referees among the several branches of the federal government, between the federal and state governments and between government at any level and the individual, corporation, association, etc. Thus, the courts are sometimes necessarily in the business of challenging the power of other organs of government. Moreover, in our constitutional system it is the courts that, for practical purposes, speak with ultimate authority on these powerful questions. The legislature is not free, as it is in the statutory case, to overturn a judicial decision of constitutional magnitude with which it disagrees.

A number of consequences follow from these relationships that bear upon the nature of effective advocacy in constitutional cases. Perhaps the most important of these is the recognition that most judges have some political/philosophical belief system in the context of which decisions in individual cases will be made. That is not to say, of course, that the political affiliation or views of a particular judge will dictate her decision in a case before her. Nonetheless, one would expect, for example, that a judge who takes seriously the concerns of federalism—who believes that the states have a major role and responsibility in the American system of government—would approach a case in which the issue involved the power of a state to undertake a particular project or program or to further its public policy, in a somewhat different fashion than one who believes that national policies are likely to provide better solutions to public problems and that the states are largely anachronistic remnants of an earlier time. Similarly, a judge who values the democratic process will be more likely to defer to the legislative branch than one who is more immediately concerned with the results of that process. A judge's philosophical bent influences the manner in which she approaches particular issues in particular cases.

The moral of all this is two-fold. First, know thy court. It is important to be aware of the political philosophical concerns of the bench and to address those concerns. Second, and no less important: Know thy case. It is not sufficient to be acquainted, no matter how thoroughly, with the policies underlying the particular substantive dispute between the parties. It is essential to be aware as well of the way those policies fit within the larger philosophical context and reflect the political values of the constitutional system.

So, for example, it is not sufficient (though it may of course be necessary) to argue for or against school bussing in terms of the importance of neighborhood schools or racial integration. The advocate must also be prepared to articulate the role of the federal government, particularly the federal courts, in what has traditionally been viewed as a state function. Similarly, it is not sufficient to argue the values of privacy and deterrence or the needs of law enforcement in a case involving the application of the exclusionary rule to a state criminal prosecution. Again the demands of federalism and the role of federal courts in the administration of state criminal justice must also be considered and addressed. And this is especially true if, as is often the case, the issue arises in a federal habeas corpus proceeding following a state court system's adjudication of the claim. So too, in cases in which the constitu-

tionality of some piece of congressional legislation or some executive action is at issue, the values, policies and principles underlying the separation of powers doctrine are every bit as necessary
to consider as the merits of the particular legislative or executive action.

Perhaps the most prevalent judicial concern
with which the advocate must come to grips in
the constitutional case is a reluctance to challenge the positions taken by other organs of government. Although there are exceptions, a substantial number of appellate courts still believe
strongly in judicial restraint. The degree, of
course, varies from court to court, judge to judge.
It varies even from one sort of case to another.
Nevertheless, the notion of restraint undoubtedly
plays some role in most courts in most cases.
The so-called presumption of constitutionality applied to statutes is just one example of this institutional restraint. Thus, in constitutional cases
the force of inertia—always formidable—plays an
especially powerful role.

A practical corollary of the restraint notion
for the advocate is the importance of what may be
called the limiting principle in constitutional adjudication. If the court is compelled to rule on a
question of constitutional magnitude, and especially if the ruling sought is one of unconstitutionality, the limits of the constitutional principle
must be clearly articulated. There are two rea-

sons for this. The first we have already considered, the notion of judicial restraint. That notion
entails more than the principle of deciding cases
on the least powerful grounds, more than merely
the avoidance of unnecessary constitutional questions. It also counsels that decisions be based on
narrower rather than broader grounds. For the
broader the ground, the greater the number of
future cases likely to be decided; that is, a broad
ground of constitutional decisionmaking in effect
decides a greater number of constitutional questions not squarely presented and hence unnecessary to determine.

The second reason for the need of a limiting
principal has to do with the obligation of an appellate court to provide guidance for the lower
courts within its system. In order to fulfill this
function, the reach of a particular decision must
be specified. Thus, the constitutional case requires not only that the advocate advance some
proposition that will result in a favorable decision
but should also suggest the limits of that proposition. (The particular limits suggested may well
vary depending upon a number of factors not the
least of which is likely to be the nature of the
party represented by the advocate. The institutional party, for example, is likely to seek a
broader decision disposing of a greater number of
potential cases so that it need not continue to ex-
pend the resources necessary to litigate them.)

This need to define the scope of a proposition for which one is contending is, of course, not limited to the constitutional case. It does, however, apply to such cases with particular force.

There are four methods through which the advocate can seek to solve the problem posed by the need to establish the limits of a proposition. First, one may attempt a principled limitation. Where it is reasonably applicable this method is likely to be the most persuasive. The limiting principle, just as the major proposition for which one contests, must be one which makes sense. If the nature of the case is such that principled limitation is not reasonable—and there are cases like that, as we shall see—it is better to resort to one of the other methods than to attempt to concoct an artificial or sophistic apparently principled limitation.

Second, the advocate might suggest a prudential method, one that relies upon a rule of reason. For example, a criminal defendant has a constitutional right to summon witnesses to testify in his behalf. Does this mean that a trial judge confronted with an attempt to adduce the testimony of a thousand character witnesses must permit each to testify? Obviously not. The limitations that the judge can impose without violating the constitutional right of the accused is one based on what is reasonable in the circumstances. In cases in which this method is relied upon the advocate ought at least to suggest the factors to be considered in determining what is reasonable.

Third, the advocate might attempt to avoid the necessity for articulating a limitation in the particular case. Typically, the advocate would argue that whatever limitation might be suggested, the facts of the particular case do not bring that limitation into play. This might be called the argument of the "hard-core." So, for example, in the case just put, if the trial judge had refused to permit any defense witnesses to testify, defense counsel could argue that the court need not be concerned with any possible permissible limitations on the defendant's right to call witnesses; for the facts of this case could not bring it within any permissible limitation. This violation is hard-core.

Finally, the advocate may attempt to draw an arbitrary line. This method is one that must be used with great care. In the rare cases in which it is appropriate, however, it can be very telling. It is a method that requires simply that a line be drawn. What is remarkable about this technique is that there is no attempt to justify the *particular* line; rather, the advocate suggests that some line must be drawn, that the prudential method, founded upon a rule of reason, is inadequate to the case because, for example, the context is such that certainty is an important value. Were this method to be applied to the case we have been considering (it should not be) it might result in limiting the defendant to, say, six witnesses. It is a method based on the idea that, in some instances, it is more important that there be a known rule than what the content of that rule is. If the last technique can be called the hard core method, then this method might be denominated the bright line method. In cases in which the advocate relies upon it, it is crucial that she do so forthrightly. First, judges appreciate candor, especially when it appears as unexpectedly as an admission that the particular rule or limitation is an arbitrary one. Second, a failure of candor is likely to place the advocate in the position of defending a particular rule that is simply not rationally defensible—and that is likely to cast doubt upon the rest of her case as well.

It should be obvious that, where it can be used, the principled limitation is clearly the favored technique. It provides the certainty of the bright line rule with the reasonability and policy justification of the prudential approach. It is the method reflected by the maxim, *"Cessante ratione legis, cessate et ipsa lex."* ("The reason of the law ceasing, the law itself also ceases.") Typically, it is the battle over principles that demonstrates the high art of appellate advocacy.

Whatever method one chooses, it is of utmost importance to be prepared with some limitation on what might otherwise be viewed as a position so extreme as to be untenable. Counsel for respondent (a former judge and a leading and usually superb advocate), found himself in just such a position in his argument before the Supreme Court on behalf of the House of Representatives in the Adam Clayton Powell case, *Powell v. McCormack*, 395 U.S. 486, 89 S.Ct. 1944 (1969). (The transcript of the oral argument, which makes fascinating reading, can be found at 24 Rutgers L.Rev. 193–229 (1970)). Much simplified for our purposes, the case involved Powell's challenge to the House's refusal to permit him to take the seat to which he had been elected. Respondent's argument, again much simplified, was that under the Constitution the House was the sole judge of the qualifications of its members and that the courts were without the power to review the determinations of the House. As might be expected when such a hard line position is advanced, the Court sought to test its limits.

Q: Suppose he had been excluded because of his race. . . . Would you say he would have any judicial remedy?

A: I should say, sir, in answer to that question, that the action of the House would be clearly unconstitutional.

[Note the failure to answer the question.]

Q: Would he have a judicial remedy?

A: .   .   . [H]e would not, sir.

The court continued to press, asking, for example, if there would be a judicial remedy if the Democrats obtained control of the House and excluded all Republicans. Respondent conceded that there would be judicial review. He then conceded that there might also be power to review if the House refused to seat any blacks on account of their race. Thus, he had placed himself in the position of arguing that a different result would obtain if on the one hand, all blacks were excluded on the basis of race, from that which would obtain on the other, if only one black was excluded on racial grounds. The next question was entirely predictable:

Q: How about ten .   .   . ?

CHAPTER SIX

ARGUMENTS

§ 6–1. In General

Just as there are different kinds of courts and different kinds of cases, so there are different kinds—more precisely, different styles—of argument. No one style is inherently better than any other. The choice among them must be made on the basis of which are most appropriate to the particular case. A case may present an especially attractive factual situation for one side or the other; another may fit neatly into a doctrinal framework; another may permit a persuasive presentation of public policy concerns based upon the consequences of a decision favoring one side or another.

Despite differences in emphasis among the various kinds of arguments, there are a number of principles to which the advocate should adhere in any well formulated presentation. Regardless of the nature of the case, it is, as we have seen (Section 2–2), imperative to develop a coherent theme for the argument. Once the theme of the argument has been developed, the language in which the argument is made should reinforce that theme. As Mark Twain said, "The difference between the right word and the almost right word is the difference between lightning and the lightning bug." Although no single word or sentence is likely to be crucial, the cumulative effect of the language of the argument should create an atmosphere consistent with the position advanced. An apt analogy might be to the painter; for while no single brush-stroke is likely to change the overall effect of the work, yet, when they are taken together, the totality of the strokes creates the impression sought. As Justice Jackson has said, "If I appear to overrate trifles, remember that a multitude of small perfections helps to set mastery of the art of advocacy apart from its counterfeit." Jackson, *Advocacy Before the Supreme Court: Suggestions for Effective Case Presentations*, 37 A.B.A.J. 801 (1951).

Consider, for example, a case like *Merrill Lynch, Pierce, Fenner & Smith v. Curran*, 456 U. S. 353, 102 S.Ct. 1825 (1982), in which the issue was the existence *vel non* of a private cause of action under the Commodities Exchange Act. Prior to the Act's extensive amendment by Congress, several lower courts had found an implied private right of action. Contemporaneously with the congressional action the Supreme Court had been substantially restricting implied causes of action, requiring plaintiffs to show clear congressional intent that a private remedy was to be part of the statutory scheme. Consequently, arguments in favor of the private right were couched in terms of preservation of the status quo—that is, that there was nothing to demonstrate a congressional intent to abrogate the previously recognized private action. Arguments in opposition spoke in terms of creation of a private remedy. Because judicial passivity is easier to achieve than judicial activism, each side sought to create the impression that it was the other which was seeking to get the Court to make an affirmative finding, to take an affirmative step. Each side sought to foist on the other the difficult task of overcoming inertia. The arguments were marked for one side by such passive words as "preserve," "leave undisturbed," "recognize" or "continue to recognize," in connection with the existence of the cause of action and such active phrases as "no intent to extinguish" in connection with its non-existence. The other side, of course, reversed this process using the action words "grant" and "create" in connection with the existence of the cause of action and more passive forms in connection with its non-existence.

A similar example was presented in a recent National Moot Court Competition problem in which the issue was the propriety of denying a jury trial in a patent infringement case because of the case's complexity. In such a situation, it made sense for the party seeking to avoid a jury to present its argument using technical hypercomplex phrases whenever referring to the facts of the case or to any issue likely to be presented to the jury. On the other hand, the party seeking a jury determination presented its position in as simple and straight-forward a manner as possible.

In the particular case the dispute concerned the rights to newly developed micro-organisms capable of degrading certain water pollutants, including oil spills. The issue might be stated by one side as whether defendant's three energy-generating plasmid bacterium infringes plaintiff's two plasmid bacterium, each plasmid of which provides a separate hydrocarbon degradative pathway. The other side might state the issue as whether the bug that defendant developed to eat oil is enough like the plaintiff's bug to constitute an invasion of plaintiff's rights. Similarly, one side would emphasize the *content* of conflicting expert testimony while the other argued in terms of the credibility of witnesses (which, of course, is intimately associated in the lawyer's—and hence, the judge's—mind with the traditional role of the jury).

Even in as common a case as a simple personal injury action, the party seeking recovery is likely to use language designed to personalize the case and create a "feel" for the disaster which overtook the client: "Mr. Johnson's leg was cut off in the crash." The other side will attempt to depersonalize and mechanize the situation: "The accident (rather than "crash") caused injury (rather than "leg was cut off") to the plaintiff (rather than "Mr. Johnson")." Plaintiffs say things like, "The man was killed while trying to cross the street;" defendants talk about "jaywalking." Similarly, my witnesses "testified"; yours "said."

Yet, in seeking to achieve this verbal picture, the keynote, as in all things, must be moderation. The effect to be achieved requires subtlety. Indeed, this caution is applicable generally to the work of the appellate advocate. Among the more common errors of advocacy is the tendency to overstate one's position or the support underlying it. This tendency is, of course, perfectly natural. Having lived with the case and the authorities and the arguments, one naturally becomes so convinced of the justice and analytic superiority of one's own position that opposing views are not given the intellectual respect they may deserve.

Unfortunately, the bench may not (almost certainly will not) start with the same unshakeable belief in the wisdom of that position. The court's perspective is likely to be a far more neutral one. As a consequence, what appears plain to the advocate, and without need of argument or support, may well appear to the court as a bald conclusory assertion. It is far better to err on the other side. The most devastating kind of opponent one is likely to meet in the appellate (or, for that matter, in the trial) arena is one believed by the court to be consummately fair.

Cases that reach an appellate court, especially those that reach a court of last resort, are frequently close cases. The judge deciding the case must write an opinion in which the matter appears 100% right or wrong. Nevertheless, the issue is seldom so clear. Typically, the judge renders a decision which, on balance, seems to her to be correct. The advocate would do well to remember this, especially in close cases. One who points out the pros and cons of each position (albeit emphasizing the pros and minimizing the cons) and points to a proper balance is likely to be more convincing than one who claims all virtue lies with her and all vice with her adversary.

This warning is applicable not only to the arguments one advances but equally to the language in which those arguments are formulated. It has been found that words intended to intensify the notions they modify—words like "definitely," "very," "clearly"—often have precisely the opposite effect. The same can be said for attempts to add emphasis through the use of variant typeface (bold face, italics, etc.). A well-crafted sentence or paragraph achieves its intended emphasis through the arrangement of its words and ideas. The use of special typeface is often the resort of the lazy or incompetent—and, perhaps equally important, is often seen to be so.

Just as the tone of one's argument ought not appear grandiose, neither ought it be strident. The allegation of bad faith, even if implicit and unintended, is almost always counterproductive. To charge the court below with bias, corruption or stupidity, through the stridency of one's claim, is almost certain to do more harm than good and is, in any event, unlikely to be accurate. Similarly, direct attacks on one's adversary rather than on her position are unseemly and make one appear less than professionally responsible. The personal attack should always be avoided.

Although there can be strong appeal to the subliminal emotional battle between the "white hats" (us) and the "black hats" (them), it is essential that subliminal is where it remains. If the case lends itself, as many do, to a good guys-bad guys approach, the emotional component of the argument, even if its driving force, must be carefully submerged within a more conventional style of argument. Moreover, it must be emphasized that both the white hats and the black hats must be portrayed as the values underlying the positions of the parties rather than as the parties themselves, their advocates or the court below.

Another common style to avoid is the hyper-technical, analytically supersophisticated approach. It will appear to many judges as hopelessly academic and artificial. The values of common sense should not be minimized. Most appellate judges are all too aware that their decisions will have significant effects on individuals, institutions and, through them, on society. Few believe they are involved in a mere academic exercise. So, although obviously one's position must be analytically defensible, analytic purity is not enough. Enough judges follow the famous aphorism of Justice Holmes—"The life of the law has been experience and not logic"—that the advocate must be able to provide a solid basis in common sense for her position.

In order to be able to do so, she must know not merely the facts of her case and the law governing it, but also the context in which those facts arise and in which that law is to be applied. Moreover, she must cultivate the ability to translate that context into the common experience—to make of it something sensible to the court. This is especially important in the policy-based argument, as we shall see (Section 6–4), but applies to other styles of argument as well.

The various styles of argument are for the appellate advocate what the toolbox is to the cabinetmaker. She must be familiar with all of them and be able to determine which are most suitable for particular tasks. This is not to say that any particular case should be argued in any single style. Indeed, most cases will require a number of different argument styles for the different issues it presents. Even with respect to a single issue, different styles of argument may help to illuminate different aspects of the position for which the advocate contends. The carpenter, after all, uses more than her plane or her hammer in creating a cabinet.

§ 6–2. The Fact-Centered Argument

There is a story told by Harris B. Steinberg, an eminent criminal lawyer from New York, about his first appellate argument for the New York District Attorney's office. The style of brief-writing in New York at the time was a clean cut division into two parts—first, "The Facts" and second, "The Law." Steinberg recounts having prepared to argue in the same style. Having completed his presentation of the facts he announced to the bench "And now Your Honor, I come to the Law." The presiding justice is then reported to have said, "Thank you, young man. You may sit down. We know the law." Steinberg, *The Criminal Appeal*, in *Counsel on Appeal* (1968).

Whether apocryphal or not the story has a moral known to every good appellate advocate. There is little worse than an advocate explaining to the court the meaning of its own opinions. As Justice Douglas has noted:

> The pre-eminent appellate advocate makes a distillation of the facts to show why the case fits neatly between two opposed precedents

and why this particular case should follow one rather than the other. It is the education of the Justices on the facts of the case that is the essential function of the appellate lawyer.

W. O. Douglas, *The Court Years* 180 (1980).

Typically the starting point of an appellate argument, oral or written, is the statement of facts. The legal arguments presented by counsel and considered by the court are in the context of "the facts." Yet, as we have seen (Sections 3–2, 3–3), the facts before the appellate court are frozen by the record made at trial. It is the way the advocate deals with these facts that is the subject of this section. Indeed, it is not too much to say that the statement of facts is itself a kind of argument.

Observe the use of "facts" in Justice Fortas's statement of the question for decision in *United States v. Yazell*, 382 U.S. 341, 86 S.Ct. 500 (1966): "The question presented is whether . . . the Federal Government, in its zealous pursuit of the balance due on a disaster loan made by the Small Business Administration, may obtain judgment against Ethel Mae Yazell of Lampases, Texas." Have you any doubt about how the Court answered the question presented?

It is the significance that one can make of the facts and the inferences to be drawn from them that form the substance of the fact-centered argument. Virtually all successful appellate arguments contain something of this argument style. It is a style directed at the law application function of the appellate court. It is the bridge between the legal doctrine and the concrete historical record both of which form the raw ingredients of decision. Thus, it is useful in any number of situations.

Perhaps the most obvious use of the fact-centered argument is in those cases in which the applicable law requires a prudential approach—a balancing of the various factors involved, followed by the application of a rule of reason. Plainly, in such instances, the decision will turn on the correspondence that the advocate can establish between the concrete facts contained in the record and the factors to be considered in assessing their significance.

Even in cases in which the doctrine does not itself call for an express consideration of the totality of the circumstances, or a weighing of the facts, the fact-centered argument remains useful. Where, for example, the doctrine to be applied is firmly established in the jurisdiction and not likely to be upset, a careful explication of the facts may make it possible to distinguish the case. Thus, if one of the parties is urging application of the well-recognized attorney-client privilege, it is unlikely that her adversary will be able to argue with any hope of success for abrogation of the privilege. On the other hand, an argument that on the facts of this case the particular information with respect to which the claim of privilege is advanced relates only to the identity of the client and hence falls outside the scope of the privilege, is far more likely to meet with success. Such an argument depends upon a precise parsing of the specific facts in the particular case. Similarly, if the law is well settled but the doctrine is relatively abstract, careful analysis and explication of the facts is likely to be critical to the success of the argument. If the rule to be applied in an action for breach of contract is that foreseeable damages are recoverable, it is the "factual" determination whether the particular damages were foreseeable that is likely to be the centerpiece of dispute. Again, a detailed explication of the facts of the agreement and of the context in which it was formed will be more likely to succeed than any appeal to doctrinal rules or principles.

Finally, where the law is clear and relatively concrete so that it is necessary to argue for some doctrinal change or for some exception to existing doctrine, close factual analysis permits the advocate to urge only so much of a departure as is necessary to prevail. The smaller the departure from existing doctrine required, the more likely the court will be to accept it. Where victory depends upon judicial acceptance of revolutionary change, disappointment is likely.

In order to present an effective fact-centered argument, the advocate must be absolutely familiar with the record facts and with their relationship to each other and to the case as a whole in all their myriad combinations. Moreover, "facts," events in the world, may be described quite narrowly and specifically or more generally and abstractly. The more narrowly a specific fact is described the less likely is it that inferences will be drawn from it. The more broadly stated, the more generalized the description, the more likely are inferences to be drawn from it. Compare, for example, a statement that the defendant's face had the same shape as the thief with the statement the defendant resembled the thief. At the same time, a number of specific facts all pointing toward the same conclusion, are likely to be perceived as more probative of that conclusion than fewer, more generalized facts. In the example just considered, if one adds to the shape of the face, eye color, the shape and length of the nose, facial hair, scars and so forth that the defendant and the thief had in common, the inference that the defendant is the thief is stronger than it would be from the general statement of resemblance. Thus, one of the skills necessary to the fact-centered argument is the ability to combine the appropriate level of generality or specificity with the appropriate number of conditions or events supporting the conclusion at which one is aiming so that the court is led ineluctably to a view of the facts compatible with the advocate's position.

A word of caution is in order here: It is one thing to use the facts in a way that highlights the reasonableness and justice of one's position; it is quite another to distort the record, to create a false impression of the facts either of the particular case or of the context in which it arose. The first is an acceptable and responsible exercise of craftsmanship; the second is professionally irresponsible. The cabinetmaker can take pride in finishing a project with a wax that emphasizes and brings out the beauty of the grain of the wood with which she has been working—but not if her aim is to camouflage gouges or scars in that wood which will show up again over time.

This skill of "working the facts" is crucial even if the dominant argument style of the advocate's presentation is to be doctrinally-centered. As Professor Reynolds has noted in a different title in this series: "The rule of *stare decisis* requires a court either to reach the same result in similar cases, or to overrule precedent. The key question, of course, is whether the cases are 'similar.' " W. Reynolds, *Judicial Process In A Nutshell* 90 (1980). Arguing that the case now before the court is similar or dissimilar to some precedent case requires a comparison of the facts of the two cases. Because, however, no two cases are precisely alike, it requires more than this. Also necessary is an analysis of the significance of any similarities or differences. And this, in turn, requires that the advocate be able to describe the facts of each case in a way that emphasizes the significance of certain facts and minimizes the significance of others.

For example, in a case in which the question is whether a demand for jury trial should be denied based on the complexity of the case and the alleged inability of the jury to comprehend it, the party seeking a bench trial might urge that a prior court had denied a jury demand on the same grounds. That party would point to the many similarities between the two cases: the anticipated length of trial, the number of documents and other exhibits, the number of witnesses and so forth. The party seeking the jury trial, on the other hand, in addition to suggesting that the precedent case had been wrongly decided, might attempt to demonstrate that in that case the complexity resulted from a large number of parties, claims, cross-claims, counterclaims and legal theories while in the case at bar any complexity there might be was concerned with the facts, conflicting testimony, and so on. Thus, it would be possible to argue that the first kind of complexity might result in a case more appropriately tried to a judge trained to comprehend legal complexity while in the case before the court there was no reason to believe the judge would be better equipped than the jury to deal with the factual complexity involved. Indeed, to the extent that the complexity could be charged to conflicting expert opinion and framed in terms of credibility, the jury might be said to be an especially appropriate decisionmaker.

There is one other feature of this argument that is noteworthy: Rather than accepting the question of her adversary, asking whether the case was too complex for a jury to understand, the advocate seeking the jury trial suggested the additional inquiry whether the judge would be superior to a jury. This subtle change in the framing of the question permitted the artful yet cogent distinction urged.

Careful preparation for the fact-centered argument requires intimate knowledge of the record, of course; but, it often requires more. It requires knowledge of the world in which the facts of the record unfolded and the ability to communicate an appreciation for the way in which that world operates. It requires, in short, the construction of a context within which the case arose and should be decided. This process is to the facts similar to what the common law process is to legal doctrine. A fabric of reality must be woven and these facts fitted within it without dropping stitches or leaving obvious seams.

This interweaving of what Professor Davis (*Administrative Law Treatise* §§ 15:1–15:5 (2d Ed. 1980); *An Approach to Problems of Evidence in the Administrative Process*, 55 Harv.L. Rev. 364, 402 (1942)), has called "legislative facts" is especially important if the advocate's presentation is to include a policy-centered argument. For without the necessary background a decision based upon a judicial assessment of the consequences or the rationality of the purposes underlying a particular position is far more difficult to obtain. In short, just as some fact-centeredness is, as we have seen, essential to a well-developed doctrinal argument, so too is it necessary to an argument rooted in public policy. Thus, in a securities law case, it may be necessary for the advocate to learn the operation of the securities markets and to communicate that information to the court to enable it to reach a sensible decision.

It is, of course, up to the advocate to demonstrate the reasons that the decision she is seeking is the sensible one. And, of course, the more specialized or esoteric the factual context is, the more important this aspect of the advocate's responsibility becomes. Judges can usually be relied upon for common sense and for knowledge of the world of the courtroom. It is rarely safe to assume specialized knowledge. Interestingly, the thoroughly prepared appellate advocate is sometimes more prone to this dangerous assumption than her less conscientious colleague and hence, must be especially alert to combat it. One can be so well prepared as to fail to realize how much more she knows than do others. Most persons with expertise or specialized knowledge that have been called upon to explain some facet of it to those not within the field have had the experience of assuming too much, of failing to understand the full depth of their audience's ignorance. The greater one's knowledge, the more one takes for granted about others' knowledge. And no one should know more about a case or the context in which it arose than the advocate arguing it.

§ 6–3. Doctrinally-Centered Arguments

Ask a civilian about the subject matter of arguments in the appellate courts and the answer is likely to be law. And legal doctrine does play a significant role in the argument and decision of appellate cases.

There is an old aphorism of conservative politics that says "When it is not necessary to change, it is necessary not to change." In most of the affairs of life the force of inertia exemplified by the aphorism is powerful. Often we do things or do them in a particular way for no better reason than that we have always done them or done them in that way.

In the law the application of the aphorism is the system of precedent or *stare decisis.* Consequently, the appellate advocate who can say that the decided cases are with her is in a powerful position. The weight of authority is heavy. That is not to say, of course, that precedent is always and mechanistically followed, that cases are never overruled. New paths are taken; but, everything else being equal, the advocate who can successfully characterize her position as the existing state of affairs and her adversary's as requiring breaking new ground or departing from existing doctrine will have an easier time persuading the court that she should prevail.

One technique by which this is accomplished is by formulating one's argument analytically or synthetically as the case may be. The analytic formulation is one that breaks down the doctrinal issue into smaller and still smaller elements, supports each element singly and thereby establishes support for one's position as an entirety. The synthetic formulation, on the other hand, eschews this fragmentation in favor of a holistic approach. Each approach has its uses.

The former is, perhaps, most successful in attempting to persuade a court that a case of first impression should be decided in a way that results in the granting of relief, the recognition of a new cause of action, compensation for theretofore uncompensated injury. Breaking the issues down into smaller and smaller components makes it far easier to find doctrinal support for each separate step. Even where this support may not be entirely convincing, it is less difficult to ask a court to take a small step unsupported than a large one.

The holistic approach, by contrast, is especially useful in resisting such a case. By compressing the issues into a single question, the advocate attempts to demonstrate how gross a departure from existing doctrine would be required to grant the relief sought by her adversary.

Consider, for example, a medical malpractice claim for a negligently performed sterilization operation, in which plaintiffs seek to recover the costs of rearing their unexpected blessing. Assume the case is one of first impression in the jurisdiction. The plaintiff is likely to argue (1) that the cause of action is one for negligence, long recognized in the jurisdiction; (2) that it is well established that all damages proximately resulting from the negligent act are recoverable; (3) that conception, pregnancy and birth are readily foreseeable consequences of the failure of sterilization. The defendant, on the other hand, is likely to argue simply that the jurisdiction has not and should not recognize a cause of action for "wrongful birth" as the plaintiff would have the court do.

Another example is furnished by a recent Moot Court Competition problem. At issue was whether the Attorney General could maintain a declaratory judgment action seeking to strike down as unconstitutional the federal Speedy Trial Act—or so it would be argued by the potential criminal defendants seeking to deny the Attorney General's standing. The Attorney General, on the other hand, would claim the power to resist speedy trial defenses in the context of motions to dismiss indictments made by defendants in criminal cases. He would further argue that any grounds, including the unconstitutionality of the statute, could be raised in opposition to the motions to dismiss. Thus, he would seek to establish first the standing to contest the constitutionality of an Act of Congress on the merits. Having done so, he could argue that the only issue left to resolve was the appropriateness of a declaratory judgment proceeding as the procedural mechanism for exercising this power.

The advocate who can analyze her case into small enough units can almost always find doctrinal support for her position. Thus, these techniques are especially helpful in cases of first impression. That is not, however, their only utility. An example of their use in a quite different context is provided by *Rosewell v. LaSalle Na-*

tional Bank, 450 U.S. 503, 101 S.Ct. 1221 (1981). At issue there was the propriety of federal interference with state taxation in light of the Tax Injunction Act, 28 U.S.C.A. § 1341, which prohibits such interference "where a plain, speedy and efficient remedy may be had in the courts of such state." Thus, the question was whether there was a state remedy meeting those requirements. Justice Brennan found that there was: The state remedy, he said, was "plain"; it was "speedy"; and it was "efficient" as envisioned by the statute. Be that as it may, said the dissenting Justice Stevens in effect, it was not "plain, speedy and efficient." The three terms, taken together, required a substantively "adequate" state remedy. Thus, the whole of the statutory requirement, for Justice Stevens, was greater than the sum of the statutory parts.

A similar approach is often used in cases in which the constitutionality of a statute is at issue. If the test of constitutionality of a particular legislative enactment is whether it serves a significant governmental interest and the government advances a number of interests it claims to be furthered by the statute, the party seeking to strike down the legislation would be likely to address each interest singly in an attempt to minimize the significance of each. The government on the other hand would be likely to attempt to cumulate the interests to magnify their significance.

And that is, in effect, the form this argument always takes. The advocate pursuing the analytic formulation seeks a simple summing of separate and discrete elements. The advocate pursuing the synthetic or holistic approach urges the artificiality of the analysis, claiming that the whole is greater than the sum of its parts.

As these few examples demonstrate, the skills of working with doctrine are important ones for the appellate advocate to master. One needs to know the law governing one's case, to understand it and to be able to communicate it. That does not mean the ability to string together a series of more or less pithy quotations from various courts or commentators supporting a particular notion. The advocate who would have her case turn upon a single word or sentence in a precedent case rather than on a close analysis of the principles upon which decision depends is not likely to succeed. Quotation is no substitute for reasoned elaboration or analytic sophistication.

Similarly, the practice of stating a proposition of law followed by a string of citations—appropriately called "trash citing"—to cases that more or less support the proposition for which they are cited is rarely persuasive. The failure to analyze or discuss the importance of the cases within the string does little to inspire confidence. This is all the more ironic given that, often, the purpose of the string citation is to impress the court with the erudition and preparation of the advocate.

Despite their weaknesses, both of those practices—one hesitates to dignify them with the label "techniques"—are common both in academic moot court exercises and in the real world of appellate advocacy. If the advocate were to bear in mind the functions to be served by appellate argument, it would be plain to her why such practices are not successful. They neither assist the court nor engender the degree of confidence in the advocate conducive to a favorable decision.

The well executed doctrinal argument, by contrast, demonstrates the way in which the principle for which the advocate contends fits within the established context of the law. It must be the result of reasoned elaboration from some rule or principle derived from some authoritative source. Thus, the advocate must show that the principle on which previously decided cases rest is equally applicable to the case at bar. An argument that calls for the application of an existing rule to a situation not previously covered by it should establish the similarities of the new situation to the old and the significance of those similarities—the manner, for example, in which the purpose of the rule will be advanced.

The application of the fourth amendment to wiretaps furnishes an example. A careful analysis of the corpus of prior fourth amendment decisions might help one to formulate a principle that the amendment is designed to protect the physical integrity of one's person, home or possessions. One might also formulate the principle that the value to be protected is privacy. Once the advocate can convince the court that the value to be served by the right against unreasonable search and seizure is privacy as well as physical integrity the extension to the new situation is a relatively simple matter. Yet both are doctrinally-based arguments; both use the precedents; both attempt to fit the case within the framework of existing law, to obtain a favorable decision without doing violence to the fabric of legal doctrine. In short the doctrinal argument is an argument from authority. Yet the strongest doctrinal arguments are those that stress the principle and reason underlying the doctrine rather than relying on authority simpliciter.

The response to the argument from authority may be: (1) The authority is inapplicable because the facts differ; (2) the authority should no longer be followed; (3) the authority stands for a different or contrary principle from that for which the advocate contends. In this last situation each party will be arguing from authority, each claiming that precedent is on its side and against the position of the adversary. Each side will argue that the opposing position is seeking to change the existing state of affairs and thus seeks to impose on that party the burden of justifying the change. For present purposes there are three categories of case authority with which we need to be concerned: the binding precedent, the nonbinding decision squarely on point and the decision in analogous but not identical cases. Each category requires somewhat different treatment.

A decision by a superior tribunal directly on point ends the case. An intermediate appellate court is without power to overrule an appellate court of last resort within the same jurisdiction: The Georgia Court of Appeals (Georgia's intermediate appellate court) is bound to follow the decisions of the Georgia Supreme Court (the state's highest court); federal courts of appeals are bound by the decisions of the United States Supreme Court as are the courts of the several states on matters of federal law. Similarly, the federal courts are bound under the doctrine of *Erie Railroad Co. v. Tompkins*, 304 U.S. 64, 58 S. Ct. 817 (1938), by decisions of at least the highest state court on matters governed by that state's law. Thus, one of the parties may argue that an earlier decision of a higher court controls the decision of the case at bar.

From time to time a lower court may anticipate the overruling of binding authority by its superior tribunal because of the passage of time or changes in conditions or for some other reason. Such an action by an inferior court amounts to, in effect, a determination that the precedent case is distinguishable from the one before the court —not because the facts of the case are different but because the social or legislative facts upon which the earlier decision was based are different. It is only in the rare case, however, that a policy-centered argument (see Section 6–4) can be used to escape from binding authority.

It is the unusual case in which it will be clear that there is binding authority squarely on point. It is expensive to take an appeal. Given the costs of lawyers, printers, bondsmen, most cases are not appealed unless there is at least some likelihood of prevailing—some relatively cogent argument to be made for each side. It is the atypical case in which it is not open to argument whether the authoritative decision apparently on point is distinguishable. And if the case before the court is not conclusively determined by the precedent case, the presence of dicta, suggestions or the like in the latter can be dealt with by appropriate argument.

The second type of precedent is the nonbinding decision squarely on point. Decisions of coordinate courts within the same jurisdiction (*e.g.*, the United States Courts of Appeals for the Second and Ninth Circuits) do not bind each other.

Similarly, decisions of courts of other jurisdictions are not binding authority (unless the governing law is the law of that other jurisdiction). The Supreme Court of New Jersey cannot bind the Supreme Court of Pennsylvania. (In some jurisdictions having multi-judge courts that sit in panels—the federal Courts of Appeals are one such example—one panel of the court is bound by earlier decisions of another panel of the same court; only the entire court, sitting en banc, can overrule an earlier panel decision. Where such a rule is applicable an appeal to a later panel presents the same situation as that previously discussed: that of the binding authority.)

That an authority does not require a particular result does not mean it can be ignored. The views of other judges that have considered the same or similar questions can illuminate a particular problem for a court and hence can assist the advocate in arguing for a similar disposition. Even secondary authority—restatements, treatises, scholarly commentary in law reviews—may be used to bolster one's position. What these sources lack in legal authority can sometimes be compensated for by persuasive force or, on occasion, the repute of the author. Restatements, for example, have no legally binding force; yet courts often rely upon them for their explication of doctrine. Thus, much of what is true with respect to the nonbinding precedent is also applicable to secondary authority.

If the authority is not merely one among a multitude of similar cases from several jurisdictions, it should not be ignored. Especially if the case is from a distinguished court or judge or if it is the only or one of a relatively few cases on point, the failure to deal with it will weaken the advocate's position in two ways. Specifically, it will make it appear to the court that the advocate cannot deal with the precedent case successfully. The unfavorable precedent may then become even more damaging for lack of a response to it. Moreover, the lack of discussion or analysis of the opposing precedent may serve to weaken the advocate's case as a whole—not merely with respect to the particular point to which the omitted authority is relevant. The failure to deal with important cases in opposition to one's own position is likely to cast doubt either upon the advocate's forthrightness or competence or both. And that sort of doubt may taint the rest of what the advocate has to say.

Whether a particular nonbinding precedent is of sufficient importance to require consideration is often a judgment call about which competent advocates may differ. The factors relevant to that judgment, however, can be articulated. For example, the greater the number of cases dealing with the same problem, the less the significance of any single such case. Similarly, the more dated the authority, especially in a field of relatively rapid or recent development, the less significant it is likely to be. On the other hand, if the opinion is written by an especially distinguished judge or decided by a particularly well regarded court, it is more likely to be given greater deference. An opinion produced by a judge considered particularly able in the specific area of the law involved in the case is also likely to be more significant, as is the decision of a court which has considered related issues (*e.g.*, commodities trading cases in the Seventh Circuit [Chicago]). In short, apart from the persuasive force of the authority itself, the external factors that make a particular authority more or less significant are of the same sort as would make one give greater credence to what some authority may have to say in any non-legal context. Obviously, the advocate relying on the decision should seek to emphasize those factors enhancing its authority while her adversary will attempt to minimize them.

If the advocate chooses not to ignore the adverse authority apparently on point, she may deal with it either directly or indirectly; she may attempt either to demonstrate that the precedent is wrong or that it can be distinguished (or, of course, both—*i.e.*, that it is wrong on its facts and also that its facts are different from those in the case now at bar). Which of those methods is most persuasive is not subject to solution through a generally applicable principle. Obviously, it depends upon the degree to which the precedent case and the case at bar are similar to or different from each other. Although it is better if one can argue persuasively that the courts that have considered the problem support one's position or at least are neutral, where the precedents are such that that argument is forced, strained and unconvincing, it makes better sense to admit forthrightly that the authority is against one's position.

Of course, that does not require the advocate to agree with the results those cases reached. Adverse decisions squarely on point that do not bind the tribunal before which one is arguing should be challenged as wrongly decided. Naturally, the advocate is then obligated to demonstrate the basis for her conclusion, as well as to state what a proper disposition would be and how the suggested principle applies to the case at bar to produce the result for which she contends. The best approach for doing so is not to build an argument critical of the precedent case. That kind of argument is necessarily negative in tone. Rather, the advocate should make the same kind of affirmative argument as would be made if there were an absence of authority on the question, while making appropriate references to the failure of the prior decision to take into account the points being made. Such an approach, while building an affirmative case for one's own position, also quite naturally undercuts and minimizes the effects of contrary authority.

§ 6–4. Policy-Centered Arguments

The policy-centered argument is among the most common styles of legal argument. It begins by positing an end to be achieved or a consequence to be avoided and then argues that a particular rule of law is a necessary or desirable means of achieving that end or avoiding that consequence. That rule of law, of course, when applied to the case at hand results in victory for the advocate's position.

There are two steps in the formulation of this style of argument. First, the goal to be achieved must be articulated; second, the advocate must demonstrate the way in which her proposed ruling will further that end. The connection between the ruling for which an advocate contends and the values she claims will be furthered by it may be based on factors as various as the possible rulings in the universe of cases. It is possible, however, to classify, at least to some extent, the kinds of values or ends that can form the basis of the argument from purpose.

There are a number of different sorts of values that one may invoke as desirable ends. Most obvious, and perhaps most appealing are those values rooted in the Constitution. To persuade a court that acceptance of an advocate's position will further freedom of speech or religion or that it will enhance the right to vote or that it will further some other constitutional value, is to take a giant step toward victory.

There are other fundamental values that, although reflected in the Constitution, do not enjoy the same explicitness of recognition as, for example, freedom of speech or the press. Nonetheless, an appeal to these values as ends to be achieved by a particular ruling can be very effective. Values of dignity, privacy, freedom, equality, fairness and so on may serve as a stout peg upon which to hang an argument. Because the legal profession prides itself on its hard-headed rationality, however, one needs to be especially cautious in arguments of this kind not to appear overly emotional or impassioned. Such appeals work best when made in the context of a more technical, doctrinally-based position.

Values given recognition in the Constitution are not the only ones that can serve as the linchpin of an argument, however. In the economic sphere, for example, effective appeal may be made to values of productivity or efficiency or competition. Notice that adversaries in the same case may both rely on the argument from purpose—or more narrowly, even the argument from economic purpose—simply by appealing to different economic values. For example, while one party may claim that a particular rule, say in the field of anti-trust, will foster the ideal of greater competition, the adverse party may claim that a contrary rule will foster the economic ideal of greater efficiency.

Finally, there is a special sort of legal goal towards which an argument may be directed—special because it is content neutral. This is the argument based on the value of certainty. Everything else being equal, a clear and certain rule upon which individuals, organizations and government agencies can rely in conducting themselves is better than a rule which is likely to result in uncertainty, risk and further litigation, with consequent increases in costs and resources.

It is, however, a value which rarely forms the centerpiece of an argument, precisely because it is content neutral. Although it is no doubt true that it is sometimes more important to have a rule than that the rule be the right one, courts tend to shy away from this rationale as a complete justification for decision. For example, it is plain that it is more important to have a settled rule known by all concerned with respect to which side of the road one is expected to use than that the rule be either the right side or the left side. Yet, the obvious arbitrariness of making the choice makes courts—as opposed to legislatures—reluctant to make a choice between those alternatives, without at least attempting some other justification. Thus, the argument from certainty is usually made to reinforce other arguments advanced by a party.

There is a variation on the argument from certainty that has particular utility in cases in which some important other value is at stake. In this form the argument typically is made by the advocate seeking a bright line or *per se* rule. One might argue that a particular end is of such importance that the rule protecting or advancing it should purposely be drawn more broadly than a strict logical analysis would require in order to assure that no case is wrongly decided.

For example, if one is convinced of the importance to the integrity of the fact-finding function of the right of the criminal defendant to confront the witnesses against him, one might argue that any denial of that right should *per se* require reversal of a conviction; this despite the fact that there are undoubtedly cases in which the denial of the confrontation right has no effect on the truth value of the verdict. One would argue that, because a case-by-case analysis is likely to result in some measure of erroneous decisionmaking, and because the value sought to be vindicated is of such overriding importance, any errors ought to be made on the side of protecting that value.

Thus, a *per se* rule, serving a prophylactic purpose, should be adopted.

The kind of argument we have been considering is analytically one that says, "The rule for which I contend is a necessary (or desirable or appropriate) means for achieving a goal toward which the law should strive." There are a number of different positions that can be taken in opposition to such an argument.

Perhaps the simplest response to the argument from purpose is to challenge the desirability of the purpose forming the linch pin of the adversary's argument. So, for example, an argument in support of a rule which it is claimed is necessary to further the rights of the criminally accused can be challenged with the claim that the rule will shackle law enforcement officials and increase crime. This responsive argument may involve little more than a recharacterization of the result that the adversary seeks to achieve.

A somewhat different response argues, that although the end sought to be achieved is a desirable one, the ruling that the adversary seeks will not further that end. So, for example, to the argument that law enforcement officials ought not violate the fourth amendment rights of suspects and that the exclusion of evidence procured by such violations will prevent the abuse, one might respond that the goal is desirable but that the means suggested for achieving it—the exclusionary rule—will not have that effect. It is then, of course, incumbent upon the advocate to advance reasons for that assertion that are likely to persuade the court.

The nature of the reasoning advanced to support these two kinds of assertions—the first directed at the desirability of ends, the second at the efficacy of particular means to achieve desired ends—differ in important ways. The first is essentially a normative argument; it is an appeal to particular values. By contrast, the second response depends not so much on a question of values but on one's judgment of the way the world works, of how people behave, of how systems function. It is an argument based on the prediction of a cause and effect relationship between a particular ruling and the result that ruling is likely to have in facilitating or retarding particular values. Consequently, its persuasive force depends upon the extent to which the advocate is able to convince the court that his view of the world is consonant with reality.

Another response to the argument from purpose admits the desirability of the end posited by one's adversary and also admits that the rule proposed will further that end, but suggests other, usually less drastic, means that will also accomplish the desired goal. For this argument to be convincing it is not sufficient merely to demonstrate the existence of such other means. One must also demonstrate their superiority over the means suggested by one's adversary.

One means may be superior to another in either of two ways. First, it may more efficiently or effectively promote the desired end; second, it may promote the desired end without (or with fewer) undesirable side-effects. Again, it should be noted that the desirability or undesirability of potential side-effects is essentially a normative question while the relationship between various means and a particular end is much more a question of legislative fact.

Although treated separately here for purposes of analysis, these responses are not mutually exclusive. Not only do these arguments often substantially overlap, but they also tend to reinforce each other. Thus, to return to our example of the fourth amendment exclusionary rule, one might argue that the rule will not deter official misconduct because the effect of applying it is too attenuated from the conduct to be deterred; that even if it does achieve the desired goal to some limited extent, it has the unfortunate side-effect of freeing the clearly guilty; and that the alternative of private claims for damages against the offending officials for fourth amendment violations will promote the goal of discouraging such conduct with greater efficiency and without the undesirable consequences.

Just as one may argue that a particular decision will further a desired end, so too may one argue that a particular decision will avoid undesirable consequences, and that a contrary decision will open a "Pandora's Box" of difficulties. There are three kinds of interests that can form the content of the Pandora's Box model. There are (1) institutional consequences (floodgates); (2) precedential consequences (if we decide case A as you would have us, cases B–H will have to be similarly decided); (3) external consequences (business will be unable to function smoothly if the principle contended for is adopted).

The model argument that appeals to the fear of institutional consequences is sometimes referred to as the floodgates argument. It is a useful device to counter appeals seeking recognition of a new right or provision of a new remedy. During the 1960's, for example, federal courts were called upon to adjudicate what soon came to be known as the "school hair cases." A number of schools across the country imposed dress and grooming codes on their students, prohibiting such things as long hair on males. Some of the students brought suits alleging that the enforcement of the codes violated their civil liberties. Among the responses to the initiation of those suits was the argument that entertaining them would result in an avalanche of similar claims of little or no consequence resulting in the inundation of the courts by claims which, though frivolous, would require much time and energy to adjudicate. Similar arguments have been advanced in cases concerning the scope of post-conviction review in the federal courts. Cases in which the courts are asked to imply private rights of action based upon a statutorily imposed duty also call forth this kind of argument.

A somewhat more refined argument based on the scarcity of institutional resources speaks not to an increase in the number of cases to be litigated if the principle of decision sought by one's adversary is adopted, but rather to the increased effort necessary to decide the kinds of cases that will be brought. It is an argument especially well suited to cases involving complex factual determinations or evidentiary hearings. Consequently, one might expect to see such arguments advanced in cases seeking review of the determinations made by administrative agencies. It is an argument often combined with that based upon the expertise of another body.

Yet another variation of the argument from institutional consequences addresses the sensitivity of the sort of issue to be decided; that is, certain kinds of cases are inappropriate for judicial resolution. This variant shades into the institutionally-centered argument considered more fully below

(Section 6–6). Thus, one might argue that certain sorts of decisions should be left to the political branches to resolve. In the federal courts, including, of course, the Supreme Court, there is another variant of this argument—the appeal to comity and federalism. In this form the argument urges that certain kinds of issues are better left to state determination. In its ultimate constitutional form the institutionally-centered argument takes the form of the political question doctrine. But even without resorting to constitutional compulsion, one can argue that prudential concerns suggest restraint.

It should be noted that typically the argument from institutional consequences aims at persuading the court not to act. It is only rarely—for example, where the court's decisions have been ignored or challenged—that the argument from institutional consequences is made in support of judicial action. It was North Carolina's failure to abide by the school desegregation principles set forth in *Brown v. Board of Education*, 347 U. S. 483, 74 S.Ct. 686 (1954) and 349 U.S. 294, 75 S.Ct. 753 (1955), that led the Court to take the extraordinary measure of ordering the specific remedy of busing in *Swann v. Charlotte-Mecklenburg Board of Education*, 402 U.S. 1, 91 S.Ct. 1267 (1971). The voting rights cases are other obvious examples of this rather unusual use of institutional consequences to support a ruling.

An argument from institutional consequences addresses the potential effect of a decision on the courts; by contrast, the argument from precedential consequences addresses the potential effects of a decision on the law. The latter argument speaks to the collateral effect of the decision on other cases likely to arise in the future. Thus, it is an argument based upon a prediction about how future decisions will be shaped by the court's answer to the issues raised in the case *sub judice*.

It is an argument exemplified by such statements as, "The test that suppresses a cheap tract today can suppress a literary gem tomorrow," *Roth v. United States*, 354 U.S. 476, 514, 77 S.Ct. 1304, 1324 (1957). It should be noted that in this form the argument does not depend on the attractiveness of the advocate's position on the merits of the particular case. Indeed, it often concedes that the advocate's position in the particular case is unattractive and it attempts to turn the weakness that results from that lack of sympathy into a strength. It says, in effect: "Despite how much you may be tempted by the equities in favor of my opponent or against me, keep in mind that you are a court whose decision will become law and hence will be applied to other situations with undesirable effect." This is what is meant by the legal bromide "Hard cases make bad law."

It is in response to arguments of this kind that the importance of "the limiting principle" (see Section 5–8) can be most easily seen. It permits an advocate to demonstrate to the court how this case can be decided in her favor without requiring future cases, superficially similar, to be decided in the same way.

The argument from external consequences speaks to the effect a particular decision is likely to have on the primary behavior of individuals or institutions. These consequences may be described in quite broad terms or in relatively narrow ones. Typically, the more narrow the consequences posited the more effective will the argument be; in the narrower argument the nexus between decision and consequence is easier to perceive and accept. So, for example, an advocate who maintains that adoption of an exclusionary rule of evidence for fourth amendment violations will result in the streets teeming with dangerous felons is less likely to be successful than one who simply advances the proposition that whatever benefit is to be derived from such a rule is to be paid for at the cost of truth or that each time such a rule is applied the result will be the release of a guilty defendant.

The difference in these two variants of the argument from external consequences is not merely a manifestation of the disadvantages of overstatement; it also demonstrates the greater persuasive force of the immediate and proximate over the remote and attenuated.

There are many other examples of the argument from external consequences. In *Dombrowski v. Pfister*, 380 U.S. 479, 85 S.Ct. 1116 (1965), for example, plaintiffs sought to prevent the state from prosecuting them under a statute alleged to violate the right of free expression. They argued, successfully, that the overbreadth of the statutes and the threatened enforcement would have a "chilling effect" on protected expression —that individuals would refrain from exercising their first amendment rights out of fear of prosecution. Most evidentiary privileges are based, at least in part, on the theory that the consequence of their abrogation would be a diminution in the desired forthrightness of parties to the relationship giving rise to the privilege. (Notice that put affirmatively this becomes the argument from purpose: Evidentiary privileges work to encourage forthright communication between parties to a relationship.)

There are a number of possible responses to the argument from consequences. Perhaps the most common is the simple denial. If one's adversary claims or is likely to claim that consequence A will result from a ruling in one's favor (and, of course, that consequence A is not desirable), the simplest response is that consequence A is not a likely result of such a ruling. Overstatement of

the consequences suggested by one's adversary—
even to the point of a *reductio ad absurdum*—is a
useful rhetorical device in minimizing the force
of such an argument. "Liability for defamation
in this case is unlikely to destroy the free press
represented by the New York Times organization," can be a telling response to the argument
that liability for defamation has implications for
the exercise of first amendment rights. In effect,
it is an attempt to make one's adversary appear
to be claiming more—unconvincingly more—than
she may in fact be claiming. Alternatively, one
might argue that consequence A would follow
only if certain other conditions are met and that
those conditions do not obtain. Or one might
argue that consequence A might, in fact, result
but that consequence A is desirable (or at least
not undesirable).

A somewhat more analytically sophisticated response is to advance a limiting principle that will
minimize the undesirable consequences suggested
by one's adversary. That is, the advocate needs
to know and be prepared to retreat to the nar-
rowest ground that will enable her to obtain the
desired relief. So, for example, if one were arguing for the recognition of a new constitutional
right for the criminally accused in the context of
a capital case one might begin with the notion
that such a right ought to be recognized generally, while being ready, willing and able to retreat

to the position that it should be recognized in fel-
ony cases and finally that, at the very least, it
ought to be recognized in capital cases.   Alternatively, one may begin with the narrower ground
if it appears that that is more likely to meet with
success with the particular tribunal.

§ 6–5. Process-Centered Arguments

Process-centered arguments differ significantly
from the other sorts of arguments considered in
this chapter.   Unlike the others, process arguments, at least nominally, press a particular
methodology of decision or standard of review
rather than a particular conclusion.   Thus, this
sort of argument must always be combined with
others that lead to the particular result for which
the advocate is contending.   The process-centered
argument makes that result easier to obtain.

Perhaps the difficulty in describing this kind of
argument can be alleviated by example.   We have
already seen one such example.   The approach
taken in the statutory case considered in Section
5–7 requires that the advocate advance not simply a particular result, not simply a particular
meaning to statutory language, but also a method
of interpretation—plain meaning, legislative purpose, whatever—by which the meaning is to be
established.   Obviously, the particular methodology suggested should be that which makes it more

likely that a favorable meaning will be imputed to the statutory language.

A similar manifestation of the process-centered argument can be found in many cases that turn upon an interpretation of constitutional language. Often, a major component of the argument will involve the question of the appropriate theory of interpretation. Should the court look to the original intention of the framers, to the lessons of history, to a literal meaning of plain language, to an examination of structural relationships established by the document? These concerns, quite as much as the result, will frequently form the focus of analysis.

A somewhat different application of the process-centered argument involves the standard to be applied in reaching a particular judgment. In this instance too, example may provide a clearer picture than explanation. Again, we have already considered one manifestation of this kind of process-centered argument in Chapter Three. When an advocate argues that a particular issue decided by a lower court is one within the trial judge's discretion, or that it is a question of fact rather than law, she is arguing, at least nominally, for a higher standard of review rather than a particular result of that review. Of course, ultimately she will contend that there was no abuse of discretion or that the finding was not clearly erroneous, advancing one or more of the more substantively oriented arguments in support of her contention. But, if the court accepts the discretion label or the fact label, her job becomes a much easier one.

Perhaps the most familiar illustration of this kind of process-centered approach is the line of cases stemming from the famous footnote 4, in *United States v. Carolene Products Co.*, 304 U.S. 144, 58 S.Ct. 778 (1938). There Justice Stone suggested that different standards of review might be appropriate for legislation challenged as violating specific constitutional guarantees or as restricting the political processes or involving "discrete and insular minorities."

One application of this approach can be found in many of the cases decided under the equal protection clause of the fourteenth amendment. If the court can be convinced that a particular disparity in treatment results in a "suspect classification," the disparity is far less likely to survive review. Similarly the different levels of evaluation—from a presumption in favor of constitutionality to strict scrutiny—with which a court may measure legislative action challenged on constitutional grounds does not appear on its face to dictate a particular result. Yet rare is the case in which a particular enactment has managed to survive strict scrutiny; rare also is the statute that has no "rational basis"—that can be demon-

strated to overcome the "presumption of constitutionality."

Each of these labels purport merely to describe
a process of decisionmaking, a standard to be applied. In form, at least, they are merely the scale
upon which the competing values are to be
weighed. Yet it should be plain, even to the most
naive, that these scales begin with a more or less
heavy weight on one side or the other. Thus, to
the extent that the court can be persuaded to
adopt one advocate's characterization rather than
the other's the decision is likely to favor the
former.

Cases in which this sort of argument can be effectively used are analytically quite complex.
Each advocate will argue on two levels and also
in the alternative. Petitioner may argue that, in
order to survive, a particular piece of legislation
must be shown to further some compelling state
interest; respondent, on the other hand, may
argue that the legislation must survive unless it
can be demonstrated to have no rational basis in
furthering some legitimate governmental interest.
That is the first level. Petitioner will then argue
that the particular statute does not further a
compelling interest; respondent will argue that it
does have a rational basis. That is the second
level. Petitioner should also argue, however, that
even if respondent's characterization of the stan-

dard of decision is accepted, the particular legislation cannot be viewed as a rational approach to a legitimate interest; similarly, respondent should argue that the governmental interest to be furthered by the statute is a compelling one. That is the alternative.

What should be noted about these forms of argument is that an advocate's position on one branch of it strengthens her position on the other. In the last example, for instance, the most strongly stated argument for petitioner would be, "This legislation must advance some compelling state interest to survive constitutional scrutiny; it is not even a rational attempt to further some legitimate interest." The most strongly stated argument for respondent: "This legislation, which need only bear a rational connection to a legitimate governmental interest, is necessary to achieve a compelling interest." Similar forms can be seen in other process-oriented arguments as well.

Oddly enough, while each branch of the argument makes the other appear *a fortiori* the case, this two-pronged approach also makes it less critical to prevail on either one or the other. The weight of the argument is divided among the two branches in a way that often serves to lighten the total—or to make it seem lighter. In large measure this is because the same substantive values that form the basis of an argument favoring one

standard rather than another also support the result the advocate hopes to achieve regardless of
the standard employed. The difference is largely
one of the degree of generality with which those
values are to be expressed. At the level of standard of review, the advocate will typically be advancing a more general application of those values; at the level of result, a more particular one.
But, because the values themselves are not essentially different, even a partial acceptance at one
level makes acceptance at the other that much
easier to obtain.

One of the appeals of this sort of argument, especially for lawyers, is its appearance of analyti-
cal and theoretical sophistication. It is a type of
argument aimed at method rather than merely
result—or so it is meant to appear. Closely allied
to this is its apparent appeal to principled decisionmaking rather than to an *ad hoc*, result-ori-
ented jurisprudence. As we have seen, the reality is quite different. Nonetheless, the forms continue to have an appeal.

§ 6–6. Institutionally Directed Arguments

Closely related to the process-centered arguments considered in the last section are arguments based on the role of the court as an institution among other institutions—more particularly on the relationship between the court and
those other institutions. These relationships

vary to a considerable extent depending upon the particular court before which the advocate is appearing; so, in consequence, does the context of this kind of argument. Its underlying theme, however, is not significantly affected. Because the variety and complexity of these various relationships are most apparent when the forum is the Supreme Court of the United States, that forum provides perhaps the best focus for discussion.

The particular institutional concerns implicated by any case depend, of course, on the facts of that case. If the validity of federal legislation is at issue, the notion of separation of powers, legislative supremacy and the relation of the judicial branch to the Congress are at the center of institutional concern. If review is sought of a decision of a lower federal court the supervisory role of the Court and its relationship to other courts within the system may be implicated. If review is sought of a decision of a state court or with respect to the constitutionality of state law, principles of federalism, of the relationship between state and national governments, will be involved. In each instance the institutionally directed argument is one whose appeal is to the role of the court in the context of the sort of controversy presented to it.

In each case, one advocate will counsel restraint—that the Court ought not second guess the assessment of other responsible institutional actors—while the other advocate will argue for the affirmative exercise of judicial power. The presumption of constitutionality, so-called, applied to congressional legislation is but one example of the institutional argument. It appeals to the notion of the legislature as the embodiment of the democratic principle whose policy determinations ought not be overridden without very substantial reasons. It is an argument that seeks, at least implicitly, to define the roles of the judicial and legislative branches in a particular way. The answering institutional argument is also directed at the roles of the two branches. It emphasizes, however, the judicial responsibility of checking unwarranted legislative power. Thus, one advocate argues for restraint; the other for a more active judicial role. Each, of course, may seek to limit the institutional position for which she contends by pointing out the reasons that make the particular case especially appropriate for judicial intervention or judicial deference.

It is not only in the cases in which a court is called upon to determine the constitutional legitimacy of some legislative enactment that these separation of powers concerns are involved. Other kinds of legislative activity may also raise significant institutional concerns. We have already seen one example of such a case in Section 5–8. *Powell v. McCormack*, 395 U.S. 486, 89 S.Ct. 1944

(1969), was a case about which it might be said that the institutional concerns were dominant and the arguments in the case clearly reflected those concerns.

Because the Constitution is the blueprint of our government, and hence ultimately defines the relationships among the institutions of that government, many of the cases suitable for institutionally directed arguments are likely to be of constitutional dimension.   But institutional arguments may be used effectively in other cases as well. Each time a court is called upon to interpret a statute institutional concerns of this kind will be present.   The theory of interpretation employed by the court, the extent to which the court feels bound by statutory language or free to make an independent judgment of legislative policy or purpose, all these reflect a particular view of the court's role with respect to that of the legislature.

Moreover, the judicial and legislative branches are not always the sole institutional actors in cases raising questions concerning separation of powers.   Cases may involve the relationship between the executive branch and the other branches as well.   For example, cases in which questions of foreign policy or international relationships are involved may be argued to be better left to executive decision;   at least, it may be argued that the views of that branch should be paid substantial deference for institutional reasons. Institutional competence also plays a major role in arguments counseling deference to administrative agencies. Arguments about whether exhaustion of administrative remedies should be required are similarly focused in large part on institutional considerations. Indeed, the availability and competence of other decisionmaking bodies will often suggest an institutionally-centered argument.

Some cases raising institutional concerns within the federal system may not directly involve the judicial branch at all. The question of the validity of the legislative veto, *Immigration & Naturalization Service v. Chadha*, —— U.S. ——, 103 S.Ct. 2764 (1983) was just such a case. It involved the relationship between the legislative and executive branches. Other examples of such institutional relationships are those cases in which the court must determine the extent of regulatory power to be exercised by an executive agency under a particular statutory scheme.

Some cases may call into question the role of the federal government vis-a-vis the states. The underlying institutional concerns are quite similar to those just considered though, of course, the institutional relationships are not the same. An example of this sort of case might be one in which the issue is whether a particular state statute has been pre-empted by federal legislation.

In that sort of case the judicial role is not implicated but the federal role is; that is, the institutional concerns focus on principles of federalism
rather than separation of powers. Obviously, the
answers will depend to a considerable extent upon
the value to be ascribed to state sovereignty as
opposed to the perceived need for federal power.
The arguments should reflect those concerns.

The same concerns are present when the issue
is whether the doctrine of *Erie Railroad Co. v.
Tompkins*, 304 U.S. 64, 58 S.Ct. 817 (1938), requires the application of state common law or
whether the case is to be controlled by a federal
rule of decision. Often, in the latter instance,
some question of Congressional will may also be
involved. In such cases the advocate may be in
the position of advancing two levels of institutional argument demanding, for example, deference to Congress but not to the states or vice versa. Obviously, the arguments may become quite
sophisticated and complex and it is up to the advocates to demonstrate, in clear and simple
terms, the reasons that the difference in relationships require or support a difference in the role
the court is to play.

The final paradigm case of this kind involves
those cases in which the Supreme Court is called
upon to review a decision rendered by a state
court in which the ground of decision may be unclear. One party may argue that the decision

rests on state law grounds sufficient to support it
regardless of federal law and hence that no federal concern is implicated. If the Court agrees that
the matter is one governed by state law, it will
not review the decision. The other side may
argue that sufficient federal concerns are present,
either because the state law is inadequate to support the state court's judgment without implicating some federal interest or because state and
federal law are so inextricably intertwined as
necessarily to implicate federal interests. Acceptance of this argument confers power to review the state court's decision. To characterize
the state court's decision convincingly as one
resting on state or federal grounds requires a
careful and precise analysis of the underlying interests at stake. Merely playing a label game is
simply not adequate.

Closely related to the institutional concerns of
federalism that arise when the question involves
the appropriate source of the law to be applied
are those raised by the cases in which the source
of law is clear but the forum for deciding, interpreting or applying that law is called into question. These cases are of two kinds: In the first
the law to be applied is federal; in the second
state law is to control. An example of the first
might present a situation in which a federal court
is asked to interfere in a proceeding in progress
in a state court because some federal right is im-

plicated by the pendency of the state litigation. Unless the circumstances are extraordinary, the demands of comity—an institutionally oriented label if there ever was one—require that the federal court refuse to intervene. The arguments in such cases invariably posit the federal courts as the primary defender of federal rights on the one hand, while on the other it is claimed that the state courts are every bit as capable and as dedicated to these federal rights so that there is no institutional superiority in the federal court warranting the sought after infringement of state sovereignty interests. *Younger v. Harris*, 401 U. S. 37, 91 S.Ct. 746 (1971), provides an excellent example of the way these institutional concerns can form the basis of a strong appellate argument. To be sure, concerns other than the purely institutional are present in such cases; but that can be said of virtually all the cases we have been considering. It is the very rare case indeed that is suitable for only one style of argument.

Similar concerns can be seen in cases in which federal courts are asked to reconsider cases governed by federal law but already decided by the state courts. Typically, principles of *res judicata* and collateral estoppel are sufficient answers to such demands. Yet, where the issue is the validity of a state court's judgment of conviction in a criminal case raising federal constitutional issues, federal habeas corpus review may be available.

Even here, however, because of the institutional demands of federalism, some deference to the state courts' determinations, at least with respect to the facts, continue to operate. Moreover, for similar institutional reasons, the state courts must first be given the opportunity to pass on the federal claims and attempts to subvert the state process will result in federal judicial refusal to entertain the claims. The institutional concerns reflected by this doctrine are laid bare in cases such as *Wainwright v. Sykes*, 433 U.S. 72, 97 S. Ct. 2497 (1977).

The second group of cases are those in which state law supplies the rule of decision. Much of the *Erie* doctrine is based upon institutional concerns. Matters about which there is no federal interest ought to be left to the states. And because the state courts are part and parcel of the state governmental system, state common law should be as operative in such cases as state statutory law. Thus, federal courts called upon to decide such questions must look to state decisions for authority. Moreover, even in the absence of authoritative state judicial pronouncements, the federal court is not free to make its own determination of policy but must attempt to decide as it believes the state court would decide. Ironically, this may make it easier to obtain a decision overruling or narrowing doctrine established by earlier state decisions in state court than in federal (see Section 4–3).

As can be seen from the foregoing, institutional concerns may be present in a wide variety of cases and manifested in a number of different contexts and combinations. The doctrine that equity will not intervene where there is an adequate remedy at law is, at least in part, a garden variety example of institutional concerns. Cases like *National League of Cities v. Usery*, 426 U.S. 833, 96 S.Ct. 2465 (1976), in which the constitutionality of applying federal wage and hour legislation to employees of state governments was at issue, raise similar institutional concerns. In a case like *National League of Cities*, these concerns are far more sophisticated and complex than most, calling into question the role of the Court with respect to congressional legislation as well as the role of the federal government vis-a-vis the states. What is crucial for the advocate is that regardless of the complexity or simplicity of the institutional interests, they must not only be identified but also analyzed, so that the reasons that these concerns lead to a favorable decision is clearly demonstrated. It is not enough merely to appeal to institutional labels without also justifying the application of those labels.

It is relatively unusual that the institutional argument alone, however weighty, will be sufficient to carry the day. The first rate advocate will

also attempt to demonstrate that the ultimate result to be obtained by deferring to institutional
constraints is independently wise and proper.
For example, where the legitimacy of a statute is
in question, one should not merely argue that the
statute is within or without the power of the legislature to enact, but also demonstrate the wisdom or caprice of the policy furthered by the
statute.

CHAPTER SEVEN

THE APPELLATE BRIEF

The most important distinction between the brief and the oral argument is that the former can be studied at leisure while the latter is a one-time thing. Thus, much of the substance and effect of oral argument is likely to be lost between the time of the argument and the time when the case is decided and an opinion drafted and agreed upon. The court peruses the brief in its own time. Because of the continued accessibility of the written argument, it can provide the working material for the court's opinion. Finally, unlike oral argument, the court cannot interrupt or derail the argument the advocate presents in her brief. The brief is the advocate's opportunity to present her case in her own way; she is in complete control of the structure of the argument and can present it to its best advantage.

It may appear somewhat odd that in this chapter devoted to the written brief there is no separate discussion of the largest portion of that document: the argument. The reason for the omission is that the basic principles of developing a persuasive argument do not differ with the medium in which the result is presented. Whatever differences or peculiarities exist in the brief or oral argument are discussed in the relevant sections and the broad rhetorical devices already discussed are major contributors to the persuasive force of an argument and need not be reiterated here. Thus, this chapter presents those ideas or suggestions of which the advocate *qua* brief writer should be cognizant.

§ 7–1. Formalities and Conventions

All courts impose certain requirements of form on documents submitted to them, including appellate briefs. It is critical that counsel adhere to these requirements. Failure to do so may result in the court's refusing to accept the submission. That, in turn, requires that the brief or at least portions of it, be redone in proper form. And, if as is often the case, counsel has waited until the last moment to file, it may result in the documents not being filed at all.

At the very least, improper form, like spelling mistakes and typographical errors, suggests to the court a lack of workmanship that may cast doubt upon the validity of the substance of one's argument. Moreover, apart from the formal requirements imposed by court rule, there are certain conventions which one should also observe. Appropriate type size, font, use of headings and sub-heads, citation form and so forth are often determined by practice. It behooves the advocate to learn the practice in the jurisdiction. It helps to demonstrate to the court that one knows what she is about.

The formalities and conventions are not simply arbitrary rules imposed to make the advocate's professional life difficult. Rather, they serve to make the judge's professional life easier. And a demonstrated consideration for the convenience of the bench is a not insignificant virtue in an advocate.

So, for example, if the Questions Presented section of a brief is customarily (whether by rule or practice) found at a certain place in the brief, a judge seeking it knows where to look. Placement elsewhere can be irritating and distracting; locating it will take some time and effort—if the judge takes the trouble. She may simply turn to the adversary's brief for her version of the Questions Presented.

Similarly, the physical layout and appearance of the brief ought to facilitate comprehension of its contents. Margins should conform to court rule or, in the absence of standardized rule, should leave sufficient white space to be comfortable for the reader. Paragraphing should also reflect concern for the reader's comfort. Paragraphs should be of sufficient length so as not to make the argument appear fragmented, but not so long as to intimidate the reader. Masses of textual material unbroken by paragraphing, sub-heads or other devices to increase white space can put off even the most interested reader.

Idiosyncratic use of language is also a distraction to the reader. In this book, for example, the feminine pronoun "she" has sometimes been used to include both male and female rather than the more conventional "he." Most readers find it jarring. It is one thing to use such devices intentionally and with the purpose of obtaining a particular effect. In the absence of such a motive— and such devices are rarely successful—the primary result is to distract the reader from what is being said. One may pay a price for originality.

Even such apparently trivial matters as citation form can be important. Unconventional citation of authorities may make it more difficult for the court to discover the sources of the argument advanced. In addition, it may prove distracting, breaking a judge's concentration on a particular line of argument at the obvious cost of the advocate's ability to persuade. At the very least, it conveys an impression of sloppiness, indifference or ignorance.

As appellate dockets grow and cases become more complex the bar can expect more and more stringent—and more stringently enforced—form requirements designed to make the work of judging more efficient. Such devices as color-coded brief covers (e.g., blue for petitioner, red for respondent, as in the United States Supreme

Court), prescribed order of the various sections of the brief and prescribed forms for title pages and covers are likely to come into increasing usage. The advocate must learn of and adhere to the particular requirements of the court before which she is to appear.

There is one formal requirement imposed by most courts with which we have not yet dealt. It is often the most difficult rule of all to follow: page limitations. By the time one has invested hour after hour after hour preparing the case by reviewing and analyzing the record and researching the law and organizing the authorities and the argument, it is natural to wish to demonstrate the results of that work in all its glorious detail. Moreover, it has been observed that nothing is as fascinating to a lawyer as the case with which she is at the moment consumed. Page limitations imposed by court rule require that the advocate resist the urge and, even in the absence of such a limitation, it is an urge that should be resisted. A brief is more likely to be hurt by too many pages than by too few. Although it never seems so to the author, the requirement that one limit one's output may work to sharpen an advocate's presentation to the ultimate advantage of her case. Selective elimination is an essential part of the art of appellate advocacy (as it is of any art).

§ 7–2. The Petitioner's Brief

Just as in oral argument the petitioner precedes the respondent, the filing of the petitioner's brief precedes the filing of respondent's brief. (In some academic moot court exercises briefs are exchanged at the same time.) More important, a court is likely to peruse the petitioner's brief first. This gives the petitioner a great advantage. And, because judges often (though by no means always) read the briefs—or at least skim them—prior to argument, a judge's first impression of the case might well be determined by the petitioner's brief.

That is the good news. The disadvantage to the petitioner is two-fold: First, she must make her case while ignorant, to some extent at least, of the shape of the case she must overcome. This is alleviated to some degree by the opportunity to file a reply brief (Section 7–4). Second, it is up to her to overcome the greatest force in the world: inertia. It is up to the petitioner to persuade the court to do something. Moreover, the something to be done is telling a colleague (the judge of the court below) that she erred. Obviously, it is easier for the appellate court to affirm.

The problem then for the petitioner is how to maximize the advantage of her position while overcoming the inertia inherent in the status quo.

First, although true of appellate advocacy generally, it is especially the case with respect to the petitioner that her argument be made in the affirmative. A negative or responsive argument almost always appears defensive. It gives away too much to one's adversary. It appears to concede that the force of inertia is against the position for which one is contending. Too often, the advocate who relies on the negative or responsive argument appears like Canute addressing the tide. More important even than these tactical considerations, however, the negative or responsive argument at its most successful demonstrates merely the weaknesses in one's opponent's position. To say that one's adversary has not made a case for victory is not necessarily the same as demonstrating that one herself has done. And, for the petitioner, it is disastrous to leave the appellate court with the conviction that neither side has made a convincing argument. It is, at least in the first instance, up to the petitioner to move the court. The hidden advantage in urging reversal is that, ordinarily, the affirmative argument for relief is the petitioner's natural argument. One need not strain to clothe a negative or responsive argument in affirmative guise.

Despite the overall affirmative nature of the typical petitioner's argument, there are likely to arise instances in which one can foresee the probability of an opposing argument with which one must deal. The approach a petitioner should take in such a case will depend to a great extent on two things: the perceived likelihood that one's opponent will make the argument and the existence of a later opportunity to meet it, that is, whether petitioner may submit a reply brief. With respect to the first of these factors, it is important to note that we are not here talking about dealing with adverse authority undiscovered by one's adversary. We are considering, rather, the use to which authority or the facts of the record are to be put. In an adversary system there is plainly no obligation to advance, in order to refute, an argument that one's adversary may choose, for whatever reason, not to propound.

With respect to the second factor—the possibility of filing a reply brief—obviously it is less important to meet an adversary's argument in advance if one has the opportunity to do so after it is made. That is not to say one should never do so. It is sometimes wiser to meet the argument before it is made affirmatively in order to defuse it. To the extent that the argument can be integrated with the rest of petitioner's argument in a way that strengthens both, it is probably wiser not to save it for reply. On the other hand, if the argument is likely to be more telling if made separately and hence in a more focused way, it might be better to save it for reply. One note of warning, however: many jurisdictions have limitations on the length of reply briefs that are considerably shorter than the limitations placed upon the main briefs and, in any event, like rebuttal in oral argument (see Section 8–8), reply briefs are most effective when short and to the point. Thus, if the argument petitioner anticipates she may have to make is likely to be a long and complex one, thought should be given to including it in the main brief. Conversely, if one is nearing the prescribed page limitations on the main brief it may be worth considering saving a responsive argument for reply.

Because the court's first impression of the case may be based upon petitioner's brief, great care must be taken to provoke an initial response in the most helpful direction. A busy judge is not likely to give all parts of the brief the same attention—especially initially, when what she may be seeking is simply a basic familiarity with the subject matter involved. The court will look first to the questions presented, the statement of facts and the summary of argument. The lesson for the advocate—especially for the petitioner—is plain: These parts of the brief should not be slighted; great pains should be taken to assure that the nature of the case and the crux of the petitioner's position is stated simply, clearly, succinctly and, of course, with all the persuasive force one can muster.

§ 7-3. The Respondent's Brief

The shape of respondent's brief will depend, to some extent, upon its timing. In most jurisdictions respondent's brief is not submitted until some time after petitioner's brief has been filed. Thus, respondent will have had the opportunity to peruse petitioner's brief before final submission of her own. As we have noted, academic moot court exercises and competitions, by contrast, often require the participants to exchange briefs at the same time.

To say that the final version of respondent's brief may await the filing of petitioner's is not to say that its commencement should await it as well. Indeed the nature of the first several stages of respondent's work is indistinguishable from petitioner's. The basic issues will be known to both parties and the general lines of argument will be known as well.

Nonetheless, if it is available, petitioner's brief should be perused and analyzed with care. Issues that respondent may not have thought it necessary to concentrate upon may be given new importance by petitioner's treatment of them or of related issues. Conversely, problems that may have seemed significant at the outset may pale as a result of petitioner's approach.

One of the choices a respondent must make is whether to adhere to the frame of reference established by petitioner or to attempt to establish a different frame of reference. Each has its own advantages and pitfalls. The difficulty with simply accepting the context provided by petitioner is that it is likely to be more favorable to petitioner than one that respondent might attempt to establish. At the same time, seeking to establish a different context requires respondent to persuade the court of two different things: (1) that the frame of reference advanced by respondent is more appropriate than that suggested by petitioner, and (2) that within that frame of reference respondent should prevail.

Perhaps the most obvious difference between the parties to the appeal is that respondent enjoys the benefits of inertia; respondent, after all, is seeking only to maintain the status quo. As a consequence, she has whatever authority is provided by the fact that a court has previously sustained her position. Moreover, to the extent that the frame of reference in which the lower court analysis occurs is one helpful to the respondent (as it is likely to be), some of the disadvantage of attempting to establish a different context from that of petitioner can be alleviated. That is to say, respondent may elect to adopt the approach of the court below rather than seeking to impose an entirely foreign frame of reference.

Finally, and related to what has just been said, there is frequently an argument available to re-

spondent that is never available to petitioner.
The argument, put most simply, is that regardless
of any technical errors, the result reached below
has done substantial justice between the parties
and therefore need not and ought not to be dis-
turbed. Sometimes this argument can be made
quite explicitly; perhaps its most obvious doctrinal manifestation is the harmless error argument (see Section 3–2). It is, however, implicit
in many respondents' arguments. In this latter
guise it may be likened to an emotional (rather
than analytic) harmless error rule. To execute it
well requires considerable artistry. It is not, by
definition, an argument based on legal principles;
technically, it is, perhaps, not an argument at all.
Nonetheless, if done well, through a careful
choice of language, structure, mood and tone, it
can be made to justify an affirmance that might
otherwise not be had. At the very least it may
be enough to convince a court that the case being
reviewed is not an appropriate one to announce a
new principle that would require a reversal or is
not the proper occasion to refuse to follow an
earlier decision.

§ 7–4. Reply Briefs

In those instances in which petitioners and respondents do not exchange briefs simultaneously,
i.e., in which respondent's brief is submitted subsequent to petitioner's, the reply brief will have

much in common with respondent's brief. It provides the petitioner with the opportunity to meet arguments raised by respondent which had not been addressed by petitioner in her original submission or which, in light of respondent's argument, turn out to have been addressed inadequately.

We have addressed earlier the question of postponing a full presentation of a particular argument for reply (see Section 7–2). The warnings there stated bear repeating, however. First, to the extent the argument is initially made by the respondent, it is she who is able to dictate the context in which it is to be addressed. Second, most jurisdictions that permit reply briefs impose relatively stringent length limitations upon them. To the extent, therefore, that one makes a decision to leave a point or points for reply, one takes the risk that other issues raised by the respondent will have to be sacrificed for lack of space.

Like a good rebuttal in oral argument (Section 8–8), the reply brief is, first of all, short. It should not be used merely to reiterate arguments advanced in the principal brief. Rather its purpose is to respond to new arguments, to distinguish or otherwise come to grips with authority not dealt with in the principal brief or to dispute misstatements of facts or law.

Consequently, the focus of the reply brief is quite narrow. It is rare for one's adversary to commit a number of significant blunders. Thus, the reply brief will be limited to those few points it is important to make. Again, like the good rebuttal, a well-executed reply brief does not pick a series of nits. It focuses instead on the one or two serious errors central (or at least important) to the resolution of the appeal, makes the points it needs to make and stops.

§ 7–5. The Amicus Brief

An amicus curiae, or friend of the court, participates in the presentation of a case although not a formal party to it. Typically, the amicus will represent some view or interest that may be affected by the outcome of the case without being sufficiently connected to it to intervene as a party. Thus, it might be said that the amicus has the best of all possible worlds: the ability to appear and make known its views with the hope of influencing the court, without the fear of being bound by doctrines of *res judicata* or collateral estoppel.

Amici may seek to participate in a case at any stage of the proceedings from trial through final appellate review. Typically, however, they enter the case at the appellate level. This is to be expected because the concerns of amici are usually with the doctrinal consequences of a result rather than with the particular facts of a case. Similarly, while amici may participate in oral argument, the more usual practice is to make their positions known to the court through the brief. It should be noted, however, that those attributes that distinguish the effective amicus brief from those of the parties are also relevant to oral argument by amici; and those attributes that distinguish the effective appellate amicus presentation from those of the parties are also likely to operate at other levels of the litigation process.

The role of the amicus curiae has changed somewhat over the years. At one time it was typical for the amicus to be invited by the court to participate. Although this still occurs occasionally, it is far more usual for the amicus to take the initiative in seeking to participate. Where amici are invited by the court it is almost always because of the fear that the parties' positions with respect to one or more of the issues will not fully illuminate all dimensions of the controversy or because the amicus possesses a peculiar expertise with respect to the subject matter of the litigation.

When the possibility of participation by an amicus does not arise from the invitation of the court there are two kinds of determinations that must be made. The potential amicus must decide whether to participate and the parties to the case must decide whether to oppose participation. For the parties the ultimate question is, of course, whether amici will help or hurt their posi-

tions. A poor presentation by an amicus, for example, may contaminate the position of the party
nominally being supported. Similarly, the addition of amici may add to the apparent significance of the consequences of a particular decision
when one of the parties is claiming that the case
presents only narrow questions. Additionally,
the interests represented by the amici may shift
the focus of the case—the center of gravity, so to
speak—to the detriment of one of the parties.

For the amicus the decision to participate depends upon other considerations. If the only aim
of the proposed participation is a reiteration of
arguments and positions being advanced by the
parties, participation is usually inappropriate.
Unless there is reason to question the quality of
the case to be presented by the parties, all that
the amicus is likely to accomplish is to add to the
burdens of overcrowded courts. For participation to be justified the amicus should advance
some position or arguments or illuminate some
aspect of the case that the parties are not likely
to raise or develop.

The factors to be considered in determining
whether to participate are also helpful in determining what makes a good, persuasive amicus
presentation. It should, of course, have those attributes that make any brief persuasive. In addition, however, it must add a perspective otherwise not adequately represented. For example,

representatives of a particular industry that might be dramatically affected by a particular case might participate as amici to advise the court of that aspect of the case which might otherwise be insufficiently considered. The amicus's presentation should be more than an echo. It should properly take a somewhat more expansive view than the immediate parties. Often amici will seek not merely to present a different perspective but to supply information—what Professor Kenneth Culp Davis termed legislative facts—through a "Brandeis brief." At the same time, the amicus must take care not to go too far beyond the record or to ignore the procedural posture of the case.

§ 7–6. Questions Presented

The Questions Presented section is likely to be the first part of the brief a busy judge (and they are all busy judges) will peruse. It quickly advises the court of precisely the job before it. Because it is likely to provide the court's first view of the case, it is critical that the Questions be carefully drafted. This section, when combined with the Statement of Facts (Section 7–9) and the Summary of Argument (Section 7–10), tells the court what it must decide, why it must decide it and the reasons for deciding it favorably to the advocate's position. It is the entire brief in microcosm. Consequently, the Questions should be drafted and redrafted, cut and polished like fine jewels. Yet, all too often, advocates draft the Questions hurriedly, almost as an afterthought.

As is the case with every other part of the brief, the Questions should be drafted to support the theme of the advocate's case, should be clear and concise and, of course, accurate. The advice often given that the Questions should be slanted, or so framed as naturally to call forth a response favorable to the advocate's position, needs to be taken with several very large grains of salt. Of course language is a tool that ought to be made to serve the advocate's cause. But Questions that are formulated in an attempt to sway the reader deceptively or unfairly are both professionally irresponsible and counterproductive. Busy as courts may be, they are rarely stupidly unperceptive. Questions that are less than honestly formulated breach the integrity of the argument and insult the court to which they are addressed.

There are instances in which the advice to formulate the Questions Presented so as to call forth responses favorable to one's position have been taken so much to heart that the results were ludicrous: "Should a conviction that violates the defendant's constitutional rights be affirmed?" "Is a contract unsupported by consideration valid?" It should be obvious that such formulations aid neither the court nor the advocate.

There are two reasons: First, the generality with which the Questions are stated render them singularly uninformative; more about this in a moment. Second, they are so obviously biased that no fair-minded judge would be likely to accept them as, in fact, the questions presented by the case. This vice is not peculiar to the over-generally stated question. Consider, for example, one of the Questions formulated by the appellants in *Metromedia, Inc. v. City of San Diego*, 453 U.S. 490, 101 S.Ct. 2882, 126 Landmark Briefs and Arguments of the Supreme Court of the United States 491, 542 (1981): "May the police power of the City of San Diego be utilized, consistently with the Fourteenth Amendment to the United States Constitution, to eliminate and totally destroy the legitimate and lawful business of outdoor advertising within San Diego?" A question so formulated informs the court of the nature of the case. Yet, the bombast with which it is framed is likely to alienate any court to whom it may be presented. An advocate who prevails with a question so stated does so in spite of, not because of, its effect.

Compare with appellant's statement of the issue just quoted that of the United States, appearing as amicus curiae, in the same case: "Whether a municipal ordinance, adopted to improve the appearance and economic condition of the city and to promote traffic safety, that generally bans the construction or maintaining of billboards advertising activities occurring off the premises on which the billboards are located, violates the Fourteenth Amendment because it is in excess of the city's police power." Without knowing any more about the case, which formulation of the issue do you think a court would be likely to find a more credible statement of the question presented by the case? And this, despite the clear direction in which it points. It may be permissible for Justice Fortas to say, as we have seen, "The question presented is whether, in the circumstances of this case, the Federal Government, in its zealous pursuit of the balance due on a disaster loan made by the Small Business Administration, may obtain judgment against Ethel Mae Yazell of Lamposas, Texas," but the wise advocate would do well not to emulate him—at least in this instance.

As has been suggested earlier (Section 2–3) it is a mistake to present too great a number of issues. A few well presented issues stand a far greater chance of sympathetic treatment than does a long list of nit-picking complaints over relatively inconsequential details. (This is, if anything, even more sound with respect to oral argument, but is important advice to the brief-writer as well.) The finely honed question, reciprocally supportive of the theme the advocate has chosen, helps to focus the minds of the court on those aspects of the case upon which the advocate's argument rests. In the rare case in which a number of important questions must be raised, they can generally be combined to form a more general question in a way that allows each aspect of the problem to reinforce the other aspects. The analysis into its more concrete components may then be accomplished either in the structure of the argument itself or through the use of sub-issues. In general, however, a few issues cogently presented are likely to be much more effective than a plethora of minor technical complaints. One should use the rifle rather than the shotgun.

Having determined the issues with which she wishes to deal, the advocate must then put those issues into a form suitable for the brief. It is important that the issues to be decided be set out in a way that permits a busy court readily to comprehend the problem it must resolve. Thus, the brief-writer should eschew long, complicated questions qualified by subordinate clauses. If it is necessary for one unfamiliar with the case to diagram the sentence in order to understand the question, it is too complex. Often some of the details need not be included within the Questions Presented section of the brief but may be left safely to the Statement of Facts or the Argument.

For the same reasons, the language of the Questions Presented should convey as much information in as little space as is practicable. Short words are better than polysyllabic linguistic units—at least when the former do not sacrifice meaning.

Perhaps the most difficult determination for the brief-writer in formulating the Questions Presented is the appropriate degree of abstraction or concreteness. Again, the best guide is whether the question as framed will assist the court in understanding what the case is about. There are two stages to the problem of abstraction/concreteness. First is the elimination of the extreme ends of the continuum which are never an appropriate conceptual level; second is the far more subtle determination of the appropriate point within the narrower band remaining. The experienced professional passes through the first stage automatically; the neophyte may have to deal with it consciously.

The examples presented earlier, in addition to suffering from the vice of bias are also, obviously, either too generally or too specifically framed to be helpful. If the Questions Presented, when transformed into declarative statements would amount to no more than legal truism—"a contract must be supported by consideration," "an unconstitutional conviction cannot stand"—that is a sure sign that they are too generally framed. Similarly, concepts used without a context (unless the context is plain) are symptomatic of overgenerality.

For example, a recent National Moot Court Competition involved the question whether the federal securities statutes were applicable to investments in commodities futures. It was not uncommon to see the Question Presented framed as "Is a commodities futures contract a security?" Unless the reader already knows a fair bit about the case, a Question so framed is singularly uninformative. And it must be emphasized and recalled that one of the major purposes of the Questions is to provide the court with as much information as possible about the nature of the case and the task of the court. Consider how much more information is conveyed by "Is an investor in commodities futures entitled to the protection of the federal securities acts?" Notice also the words "investor" and "protection" which are associated with the federal securities laws by lawyers familiar with that area. Thus, because these statutes are designed for investor protection, the use of these words begins to carry the court to an affirmative response.

The adversary's formulation of the same issue might be "Should the federal securities laws be extended to speculation in commodites futures?" Notice the absence of the words "investor" and "protection" and the use of such words as "extended" and "speculation." "Extended" suggests that the court is being asked to go beyond what the legislature has provided; "speculation" has obvious negative connotations. Both versions of the Question, however, inform the court of the nature of the underlying controversy; neither is unfairly slanted.

The converse problem may also surface: formulating Questions that are too concrete, that include too many of the particulars of the case. The flaws here are that the court has difficulty determining the crux of the case. It may believe it is being asked to indulge in *ad hoc* rather than principled decisionmaking. The Questions must be sufficiently abstract that an answer to them will produce a principle capable of deciding not only this but also other similar cases. So, for example, any reference to the parties should reflect their roles in the case to be decided with respect to the issues the court is asked to resolve; thus, in the foregoing example, "investor" not "petitioner" and certainly not "Smith." A question must be so formulated that, when stated declaratively, it results in a principle of law. In large part, then, the breadth or narrowness, the abstractness or concreteness, of the principle depends upon how broad or narrow a decision the advocate is seeking, balanced against the likelihood of obtaining a favorable ruling.

It is generally the case that the advocate seeking a change in the law or its application stands a better chance of victory the less sweeping the change she advocates. Stating the Questions Presented concretely may narrow the issues sufficiently to increase the likelihood of success. On the other hand, the advocate resisting the change may state the Questions quite broadly, suggesting that any change wrought by the decision will be sweeping.

§ 7–7. Front Matter

Often regarded as inconsequential by appellate advocates is the front matter of the brief: Cover, Table of Contents, Table of Authorities and similar sections that may be required by particular courts. Because this material is rarely of substantive significance it is often postponed until the last moment and then delegated to clerk or secretary. At least some of the postponement is, of course, necessitated by the need to include page numbers which are not available until the substantive work on the brief is completed. More of the delay, however, is the result of procrastination of a dull, uncreative and thankless task.

Nonetheless, it is important work for a number of reasons. First, no part of a brief submitted to an appellate court should be regarded as inconsequential. Second, at least some parts of the front matter of the brief do have substantive impact. The Table of Contents, for example, indicates the main lines of argument to be followed by the brief; it reveals the structure of the case over which the effective advocate will have labored long and hard (Section 2–3). It makes clear the relationships among the various ideas and doctrines incorporated into the argument. It makes clear which points are most important and which are subordinate, as well as to which they are subordinate. The Table of Contents—more specifically the propositions or argument headings and subheadings contained in it—is (along with the Questions Presented, Statement of Facts and Summary of Argument) among the most important elements of the brief. And the busier the court, the more important are they likely to be.

Even the Table of Authorities can reveal much about the advocate, especially the thoroughness of her preparation and research. The absence of important material from the Table of Authorities reveals either of two things: if the omitted material is actually relied upon in the brief, the advocate is sloppy; if excluded altogether, the advocate is very likely less than thoroughly prepared. On the other hand, if the Table of Authorities includes all the relevant material the impression on the court is likely to be far more favorable.

This is obviously more important when the bench is familiar with the issues involved; and the more familiar with them the court is, the more important it becomes. This familiarity may be the result of prior decisionmaking by the court, of scholarly publication by one of its members, or of having perused one's opponent's brief. Thus, if one's opponent has made a cogent argument based upon a particular case or line of cases, the bench may turn first to one's Table of Authorities to discover where in the brief that argument is met. And if that authority is not included in one's own Table of Authorities, the court is likely to assume that it has been overlooked or, worse, that it cannot be met or is conceded. It is important to note here that even if the substance of the argument is adumbrated in the body of the brief the court may have already turned its attention away from that particular element of the case by the time it arrives at that point in the brief. A complete Table of Authorities should enable the court to find the treatment of particular authority with instant ease.

Finally, imagine, if you will, the likely reaction of the judge who has herself written in the area in which the case arises and who fails to find that writing in the Table of Authorities of one side. It is important to be thorough, careful and complete, not merely in doing the necessary research but also in having that care reflected in the Table of Authorities.

The combination of the Table of Contents, indicating the pages where the reader will find particular propositions or arguments developed, with the Table of Authorities, indicating the lo-

cation in the brief of the authority upon which
the advocate relies, reveals to the court the relationship between the argument and the authority for it. Thus, well prepared front matter
should enable the court, before turning to the
body of the brief itself, to determine the main
lines of the advocate's argument, what is subordinate and what is major and what authority is relevant to the positions advanced.

Even apart from the substantive effect of taking
pains with the front matter, such precision demonstrates the care and integrity upon which the
court's acceptance of the advocate's position is at
least in some measure based. Similarly, front
matter that is well-executed makes the job of the
court easier and will be appreciated. Finally,
neat and physically well laid-out front matter often constitutes the court's first impression of the
advocate and that impression ought to be favorable. Thus, dots connecting page numbers to the
material appearing at those pages should be
aligned vertically and horizontally; care should
be taken to use appropriate type style, citation
form, margins and indentations. Material indexed
to particular pages should appear at those pages.
Authorities should be designated by category (*e.
g.*, cases, statutes, treatises, etc.) as prescribed by
court rule or local practice.

Any single error with respect to these elements
of the brief or with respect to any item within

these elements is, of course, unlikely to lose one's case. Nonetheless, each stroke of the brush contributes to the picture the advocate is attempting to paint; everything—everything—in the brief contributes to the effect it will have on the bench. One therefore ought to strive mightily to assure that that effect is positive. Even if we cannot do the great tasks as well as we would like, surely we can take pains to assure that the smaller tasks are done as they ought to be.

§ 7–8. Point Headings

The point headings or argument headings serve two functions in the brief: an organizational function and a crystallizing function. The organizational aspect of point headings itself has two purposes. First, the arrangement of the points in the Index or Table of Contents permits the court to see at a glance the structure of the argument —the skeleton, if you will, which is then fleshed out in the argument itself. Second, a point heading serves to direct the reader to that part of the brief in which the argument on that point is to be found. Thus, to the extent that an argument is complex, containing a number of subordinate notions that are nonetheless necessary for a development of the advocate's position, sub-heads can be a useful means of assisting the reader to comprehend the argument.

If these organizational functions were the only load to be carried by the point headings, they would be important but relatively simple to draft. Topical captions would serve the purpose adequately. Indeed, many advocates rely on topical headings alone. To do so is to discard the second critical function of the point headings—the persuasive function. Well-drafted point headings should distill for the court the essence of the advocate's argument. They should be revised and polished until they express the crux of the advocate's position on each aspect of the case necessary to victory.

For example, in a garden variety automobile accident case which included a defense of contributory negligence, the argumentative point heading might be, "Plaintiff's failure to use passenger restraints as required by statute (citation) constitutes contributory negligence barring his claim"; the topical caption would amount to little more than "contributory negligence."

As is true of the Questions Presented, the most difficult aspect of drafting point headings is determining the appropriate level of abstraction. The inclusion of too many facts makes the argument appear too concrete, seeming to call for an *ad hoc* decision, and hence to be unprincipled; too few facts and the headings are insufficiently informative and, generally, so obviously true as to be unpersuasive in the particular case. In our automobile accident case, for example, such a heading might be, "Contributory negligence bars recovery." Although obviously true the purpose of that section of the brief is not to persuade the court of the validity of the rule (at least, so one hopes) but to demonstrate its application in the particular case. The mere statement of black letter law fails utterly in this respect. Interestingly, the too broad assertion seems to be more common than the too specific one, perhaps because it requires less thought and effort. The additional time and trouble it takes to formulate well-crafted, convincing argument headings pay handsome dividends, however, and is a wise investment indeed.

Often appellate advocates will formulate the point headings of the brief to mirror the questions presented; that is, the questions and the points will be identical save that the former will be framed interrogatively and the latter declaratively. The only virtue—if it can be called that —of such a practice is the saving of time and intellectual energy for the brief writer. In terms of effective advocacy, however, it is decidedly not good practice. A moment's reflection should reveal the reasons. The Questions Presented provides one opportunity to arrest the attention of the court and begin the process of persuasion by artful expression. The point headings provide an additional opportunity to do so. If the same mode of expression is used for both sections, what had been two opportunities becomes only one. Obviously the effective advocate ought not forfeit any opportunity to persuade.

That is not to say, however, that the point headings and the Questions Presented should be entirely unrelated. They should both, for example, follow the organizational structure of the brief. How, then, should they differ? The answer lies in our previous consideration (Section 7–6) of the appropriate level of abstraction. As has been suggested, after the two extremes on the continuum from specific to abstract formulation have been eliminated, there will remain a more or less significant range of abstraction within which to conduct the argument. The point within this range on which the advocate elects to focus is subject to a number of strategic and tactical factors, including the breadth of the rule she is pursuing and the degree to which she believes the court is willing to break new ground as opposed to making only minor modifications to existing doctrine. (Not the least important factor is the long range interest represented by the advocate; the individual client may be seeking relief only in the particular case and a narrow rule covering the particular case may be all that is necessary. The institutional client, on the other hand, may be seeking a broader rule that will dictate, or at least influence, the result in many similar cases in which the institution is involved—or even will require or permit a change in primary behavior that is more significant to the institution than the result in any individual lawsuit.)

Because the Questions Presented and Argument Headings present opportunities to make essentially the same points in the same order, they allow for greater flexibility in the breadth of the decision being pursued. Thus, if the Questions Presented tend toward the more concrete, narrow end of the acceptable range of the continuum, the Point Headings should tend toward the more general, abstract end or vice versa. The argument itself may then range between them, the limits having been set by these two elements of the brief.

§ 7–9. Statement of Facts

The statement of facts may be the most important section of the brief. This is true for a number of reasons. First, all judges know something of the law. (Recall the war story recounted in Section 6–2.) The appellate court, however, knows nothing of the facts until the advocates inform it. Second, judges are human beings and, although trained in law, still strive to do justice for the parties before them—and justice is heavily fact-dependent. Finally, it is through the presentation of the facts of a case that the court becomes acquainted with the events or transactions giving rise to the litigation. Appellate judges, for the most part, have neither the time nor the inclination to wade through the entire record to discover what the case is about. The statement of facts tells them.

Like the Questions Presented, the Statement of Facts should be so drafted and redrafted as to incline the court to an appreciation of the justice of the advocate's position. Again, however, as is true of the Questions Presented, this is not to suggest a misleading, biased or slanted presentation. Even apart from the professional irresponsibility in such a presentation, it is likely that the lack of candor will be perceived by the court with a consequent distrust of the rest of what the advocate has to say. The Statement of Facts must, above all, be fair and supported by appropriate citations to the record.

That having been said, however, it is also true that there is more than one way to present a fair statement of facts. By one's choice of words, by the ordering of statements and events, by the structure of the description, one can paint subtly different pictures of the events underlying the case—and do so without distortion.

The first principle for the presentation of the Statement of Facts is that, like everything in the brief, it should reinforce and support the theme upon which the advocate has chosen to rely. The statement must also be clear and readily comprehensible to the court. Finally, the statement must include all the material facts but should not be overburdened by irrelevancies that clutter the statement and burden the reader. Above all, unfavorable facts must not be omitted but must be dealt with fully and fairly. Of course, the Statement of Facts should engage the reader—involve him or her in the human story that gave rise to the litigation. How then does the advocate go about preparing a Statement of Facts that meets these criteria?

The first step in the preparation of the Statement of Facts may be viewed as a process of filtration or selection. The record will contain innumerable facts of greater or lesser importance to the appeal—everything from the addresses and occupations of witnesses to road and weather conditions at the time of the automobile accident. The degree of detail necessary obviously will vary from case to case. Nothing should be omitted that a fair-minded reader would be likely to find significant. Enough detail should be included to provide the color and context necessary to understanding the significance of the events giving rise to the litigation. Argument should not be included. This is where the court looks to find out what happened, not to learn the advocate's belief or characterization about the quality of the various incidents.

After the salient facts have been winnowed out of the record the advocate must determine the order in which to present them, that is, the structure of the Statement of Facts. The process of determining the most effective structure for this section of the brief is somewhat similar to that used in structuring the case as a whole. The most important criteria in determining the structure are consistency with the theme and structure of the argument and coherence and clarity. Within these criteria several patterns of organization are possible. As with the case as a whole, it is essential that the Statement of Facts have some coherent structure. There is little that is worse or more difficult to follow than an aimless recounting of events in no particular order and with no apparent purpose. Perhaps the most obvious as well as the most common organizing principle is chronological. One starts at the first event in time and proceeds to the next and the next and so on until the tale is told. Although apparently unimaginative, organizing the facts in this way often makes the statement easy to follow. It may not be the best organization, however, at least in those more complicated cases in which events may have transpired simultaneously, involving different persons in different locations. Nonetheless, any organization of the facts will have some chronological features.

One organizing principle that is sometimes used, though rarely effectively, is a variation on the chronological approach. Rather than recounting the events in the order of their occurrence, the advocate recounts them in the order in which evidence of them was adduced at trial. In a sense, organizing the statement in this way renders it a summary of the trial rather than a summary of the facts. This may be an effective method of presentation if the issue to be decided is a purely procedural one, although even then it is difficult to engage the reader in a statement so organized. The order of proof at trial is often dictated by concerns of convenience and logistics. For example, the plaintiff's first witness may testify to facts within his knowledge that transpired at time one and time four and may then be asked to authenticate a document whose importance may not be apparent until plaintiff's fifth witness has testified. This is necessary to avoid excusing and recalling and excusing and recalling each witness several times. (At trial, the opening statements are designed to assist the fact-finder in placing these bits and pieces of information into the context of the larger picture.) An appellate brief which recounts the testimony of Witness One followed by the testimony of Witness Two and so on is likely to be singularly unhelpful to a judge who turns to the Statement of Facts to obtain a coherent picture of what the case is about.

Another possible organizational principle is a topical one. This method of organizing the facts is especially useful in the more complicated case. The topics around which the facts are to be organized can be varied to suit the needs of the particular case. For example, one may organize the facts according to the legal theories being advanced, by reference to the various participants in the events, by the injuries for which relief is sought and so forth.

Finally, one might choose to paint first with a broad brush, outlining the events giving rise to the litigation at the beginning of the statement and then filling in the details of those events. This format may be especially helpful when the significance of some of these details may not be evident until the whole picture is presented.

It should be noted that the several modes of organization suggested are neither exhaustive nor mutually exclusive. Almost all well-constructed statements will contain elements of more than one mode. Nonetheless, it should prove helpful to a coherent organization to be aware of the various kinds of structural techniques and to know which of them one is using and why one is using it.

In order to choose the most desirable structure it may be helpful to prepare something akin to a list of the facts to be included and then to classify each along several different continua: by witness, by how favorable or unfavorable to the position being advocated, chronologically, topically and so forth. It is also helpful to include a citation to the record for each fact listed as an assurance that the statements are supported. This will also assist in the writing of the statement.

When the general structure of the Statement of Facts has been determined, there should be an outline of this section of the brief. The advocate may then begin to fill in this outline.

Although this book is not intended as a guide to legal writing, a few suggestions about drafting the text of the Statement of Facts may prove helpful. It is well to keep in mind that the purpose to be served is to assist a busy court and to persuade it of the rightness of one's cause. The first paragraph or two, therefore, should provide a context for the reader: It should include the nature of the case and indicate the party appealing, the basis of the appeal and the identities of the parties. (In some jurisdictions a separate Statement of the Case is required. The purpose of such a section is to provide the court with the procedural history and present state of the litigation. In such jurisdictions this material would not be repeated in the Statement of Facts.)

As the particular language to be used in drafting the text of the Statement is considered, the

theme of the case must be kept firmly in mind.
It is that theme which will determine the form
and style of much of the statement. For example, one can identify the parties to the case in a
number of different ways: appellant-appellee,
plaintiff-defendant, creditor-debtor, landlord-ten-
ant, doctor-patient, and so on. The way in which
the parties are designated should support the chosen theme and should also assist the court in following the story being told. Consequently, the
parties should, as a general rule, be designated by
the titles that are critical to their roles in the
case. It is rarely helpful, either to the advocate's
own cause or to the court she is trying to persuade, to refer to the parties as petitioner and respondent throughout the Statement of Facts.
Yet those designations are commonly used by appellate advocates with little thought to the convenience of the court. To do so requires the court
to recall or turn back to determine who is who.
(Of course, if one of the issues in the case involves, for example, the burden to be borne in order to overturn a ruling by the trial court, the
roles of petitioner and respondent may be the
critical ones. In that situation those titles would
be entirely appropriate.)

Once the context has been provided by describing the nature of the case and identifying the
parties, it is time to tell the story that gave rise
to the litigation. Although the role of the brief

writer is not that of a Hemingway or a Fitzgerald, there is no need for the story to bore the reader. It should be told in a way that engages the interest of the reader—that makes her want to continue. Moreover, it should be told in a way that presents the case and the participants as real people involved in a real controversy, not as theoretical abstractions concerned with some noumenal generalization.

It should be plainly written, in short words and clear sentences, but imagery that brings the events described to life need not be avoided. (Nor, of course, should it be overdone; the dramatic phrase or statement works only when used sparingly.) Finally, the Statement should be focused and disciplined rather than aimless and meandering. It should have a beginning, a middle and an end.

After the statement has been drafted, it should be reviewed to assure that it is accurate and not argumentative. Even after the final draft has been prepared and proofread, the citations to the record supporting each statement should be checked. It is not unusual that over the course of several drafts the meaning of statements in the original changes to the point that they no longer accurately reflect the record. After the citations have been checked, the full statement should be gone over once again to assure its objectivity. This point cannot be overemphasized. Many guides or manuals on appellate advocacy suggest that the Statement of Facts should be so constructed that a court, upon completing its perusal of it, will be virtually compelled to find in favor of the position advanced by the advocate. (As we have already considered, much the same advice is often given with respect to the preparation of the Questions Presented section of the brief. (Section 7–6)) Beware such advice! If all that is meant is that it is permissible and desirable to present one's case sympathetically, the advice is sound. There is a risk, however, that the advice will be taken to mean far more than that. It is essential that the advocate be meticulous in her statement of the case. Special danger lies in the temptation to convey half truths through the use of partial statements. To do so is both professionally irresponsible and potentially disastrous to the cause for which one is contending.

The line is not always an easy one to draw. Nonetheless, the advocate must consider carefully such issues in deciding, for example, when it is legitimate to suggest a causal relation between two events by recounting them one immediately after the other, or to suggest a lack of causation by separating them by a paragraph or two. Although difficult, such judgments are part of the responsibility of the professional.

§ 7–10. Summary of Argument

Some jurisdictions require, some merely permit, the brief writer to include a summary of the argument as a separate section of the brief. In any case in which the advocate is permitted to do so, she should. It is among the more important sections of the brief and should be revised as frequently as necessary to produce a tightly-knit, persuasive statement that presents in capsule form—just a few paragraphs—the crux of the advocate's position. When combined with the Statement of Facts and Questions Presented, the Summary of Argument should provide a busy court with all it needs to understand what the case is about and the kernel of the advocate's position. Sometimes these three sections are all the judge will read before oral argument. Sometimes they will be used to refresh a judge's recollection of an advocate's position without the necessity of reviewing the entire brief. As a consequence, they must provide the hook with which to catch the mind of the court and begin to lead it to acceptance of the advocate's position.

It is the practice of some advocates to reproduce the point or argument headings as the Summary of Argument. It is, however, poor practice to do so. It adds length without adding persuasive force. The Table of Contents will reveal the point headings and their replication in a separate section is therefore of no utility. Instead the

Summary of Argument should be a concise—even terse—precis of the advocate's position.

The Summary should always be prepared after the argument section of the brief (though, of course, it will appear before it). It should be somewhat more fully developed than the argument headings but still should be a summary. Perhaps ten percent of the length of the argument itself is a reasonable goal for which to strive.

If the Point Headings in the Table of Contents can be seen as a block outline of the Argument, the Summary might be likened to a sentence outline. Although it should not repeat the precise language used in the argument, it might be viewed as essentially a compendium of the topic sentences of the paragraphs of the argument. Its organization should follow that of the argument itself.

§ 7–11. Footnotes

Appellate briefs are not law review articles. The scholarship and erudition of the author do not count and their demonstration through the extensive use of footnotes is rarely helpful to the persuasive force of the argument. It usually hurts. It is far more important to persuade than to impress. Better to have the court believe the advocate's position is strong despite the flaws in her performance than for it to believe her performance is more appealing than the merits of her position.

Footnotes break the rhythm and flow of the presentation and distract the reader from them. Often they are an annoyance to the court, requiring a constant shifting of intellectual gears. Thus, consideration for one's audience—always a dominant concern in appellate advocacy—and the demands of persuasiveness counsel against extensive footnotes. (Similarly, long or frequent quotation is usually unpersuasive; better, usually, to paraphrase the authority on which one relies.)

That is not to say that footnotes should never be used in the brief; rather their use should be carefully limited. Footnotes can be helpful in a few situations. First, a well crafted footnote can be used to suggest an argument that the advocate does not wish to develop fully in the body of the brief but which she does not wish to abandon entirely either. Typically, this will be the sort of argument that cannot be made to fit smoothly within the frame of reference of the rest of the brief—an argument that, if fully developed, would strike a discordant note. Obviously, it is not the sort of argument likely to be dispositive, although it may provide the first steps down a path that will enable a court wishing to do so to avoid deciding the difficult questions to which the main parts of the brief are addressed.

In academic competitions, such footnotes can be very useful; the problems themselves are sometimes drafted by third-year students and may not be perfectly thought through. As a result, "hidden" issues sometimes present themselves, and contestants face the dilemma of wasting brief pages and argument time on something in which the "court" may have no interest (and didn't even know was there) or of ignoring a tricky element of the problem at the cost of extra points.

In a recent competition, the problem contained just such a "hidden" issue and, because it went to jurisdiction, the bench (or the opponents) could raise it for the first time in oral argument. One team handled it in a footnote as follows:

> Jurisdiction in this action was alleged under 28 U.S.C. § 1331. Though this may be problematic, *see Skelly Oil Co. v. Phillips Petroleum Co.*, 339 U.S. 667 (1950), the district court had the power to hear this case under 28 U.S.C. § 1345, which provides jurisdiction in all cases in which the United States is plaintiff.

This is a meaty footnote: without wasting precious space in the brief, it tells the judges that the team recognized the problem, researched it, and came up with a solution.

A similar basis for a footnoted argument might be the difficulty or complexity of a position that the advocate believes is unlikely to be successful. Allusion to it in a footnote allows the court wishing to hear more to address the problem in oral argument and, perhaps, to permit supplemental briefs with respect to it. For petitioner, the argument may be further developed in a reply brief if respondent addresses it in any detail.

Another purpose a footnote may serve is to respond to an argument not (or not yet) made by one's adversary but likely to occur at some point during the appeal. Of course, even here one should endeavor to make the argument affirmatively. The mere fact that it is made in a footnote suggests that the writer regards the opposing argument to be trivial. It should appear almost as a throwaway. For example, in a federal habeas corpus proceeding in which the petitioner was convicted and appealed in the state court system but did not petition the United States Supreme Court for review of his conviction, petitioner may wish to include a footnote to the effect that he has exhausted state remedies as required and that the failure to seek Supreme Court review of the original conviction does not constitute a failure to exhaust, perhaps citing a case to that effect.

Footnotes ought not be used for any crucial step in one's argument or analysis. If they are to be used to advantage, their scope and focus must be limited to tangential or responsive points requiring little development. Plainly, the main arguments must be capable of standing alone, without reference to any notes. Finally, footnotes should be brief and there should be only those few that are truly necessary.

§ 7–12. Appendices

It should be reiterated that one of the cardinal virtues of a good brief is the assistance it provides to overworked judges. Although briefs are generally no longer brief (if they ever were), it is still true that they do not have the bulk of a volume of a reporter series, much less a law library. That is, they are portable.

This portability permits the overworked judge to use her time with greater efficiency. Briefs can be read on the train going to and from the judge's home, over morning coffee, after dinner, in bed or anywhere and anytime it suits the convenience of the judge. If the brief is to do the job the advocate wishes it to do, it must provide all the essential tools necessary to an understanding of the case. The judge may not have immediate access to the trial record or to controlling statutes or regulations or other materials necessary to full comprehension.

These factors should make the role and purpose of appendices clear. They are to supply the court with those materials necessary to reaching a decision in the case but not suited to inclusion in the body of the brief itself. It is the appendices that make of the brief an independent self-contained document.

In many jurisdictions the contents of an appendix is mandated by statute or court rule. Typically required is the opinion and order of the court whose decision is the subject of the appeal (if it is unreported), the text of applicable statutes or regulations and those portions of the record necessary to the appeal. In short, the appendix should contain all matter external to the argument but necessary to inform the decision of the appellate court. It is that part of the brief not written by the advocate but merely selected by her. This process of selection, however, should be given the same care and attention as other parts of the brief. It should not be so voluminous as to be unwieldy but should contain all necessary material. One criterion for what should be included in the appendix might be whether it is necessary for the deciding judge to read the material in question. Ultimately, however, it is the judgment exercised in selecting and excluding material to be reproduced in appendices that represents the art of advocacy as applied to this section of the brief.

CHAPTER EIGHT

THE ORAL ARGUMENT

As with all other aspects of the role of the appellate advocate, the purpose of oral argument is to persuade the court that law, justice and right favor one's position. If there is a difference in the kind of argument one might make in the brief and in orals it perhaps is this: the brief shows the court how to decide the case in one's favor; the oral argument demonstrates why it should be so decided. One consequence of this distinction is that, in a great many cases, the oral argument is concerned less with "law" than the brief. Often, especially in intermediate appellate courts, the argument is about facts: the facts of the case before the court and the facts of the precedent cases relevant to a decision by the court. In courts of last resort, policy matters often play as great a role as "law" in the oral argument. Yet, it is easy to overstate the distinction between the brief and oral argument. It is more a difference in tone and emphasis than any fundamental difference in substance.

Much has been written on both sides of the question whether oral argument retains the significance it once had in persuading the court. It has been suggested—from both sides of the bench

—that oral argument is rarely decisive and is often little more than a vestigial formality with virtually no effect on the results in particular cases; it has also been suggested, again from both sides of the bench, that courts rely heavily on oral argument. The probability is that the importance of the role played by oral argument varies widely from court to court and from judge to judge. But more can be said than that. For, if nothing else, oral argument is the one opportunity the advocate will have to rub minds directly with those who will decide the case. That alone should suffice as motivation to do the best possible job of persuasion. And that requires careful, time-consuming, painstaking preparation.

§ 8–1. Preparation

Before considering the preparation necessary for a good oral argument of a particular case, we must consider a more general kind of preparation for any oral presentation. No less an authority than E. Barrett Prettyman, *Some Observations Concerning Appellate Advocacy*, 39 Va.L.Rev. 285 (1953), has advised young lawyers never to decline an invitation to speak. Public speaking is, for most, uncomfortable—at least the first several times it is undertaken. The advocate who must argue orally to the court should be as comfortable as possible about speaking in general. The anxiety that naturally accompanies most oral argument does not require an additional feeling of general anxiety arising from the role of public speaker.

There is only one way to become more at ease while making any sort of public presentation. That is to do it and do it often. The subject matter, the audience, the purpose of the presentation is of less importance than gaining the experience of speaking in public. One can learn much from addressing a community group that will prove helpful when attempting to persuade a court.

Even having become relatively confident and at ease about speaking in public generally, however, many find oral argument the most anxiety-producing and intimidating part of appellate advocacy. A bit of this anxiety is helpful; it provides the psychological edge often necessary to good performance. It is rare, and probably not especially helpful, to go into oral argument totally relaxed and at ease. Yet, obviously, too much of this anxiety is debilitating. The most effective antidote to destructive anxiety is confidence and the only way to achieve that confidence is through preparation. Fortunately, few of us are arrogant enough to believe that we can execute a good oral argument entirely (or even predominantly) on the strength of our native genius. Consequently, the motivation to prepare is strong. Although time is always scarce, it is im-

perative that the advocate take the time necessary to prepare to meet the court.

No matter how well prepared the advocate may
be there is likely to be some unanticipated issue
or event that arises during the course of the argument. If, however, more than ten percent of
what occurs during the course of an oral argument has not been anticipated, it is a sure sign
that the advocate has not done her homework.
Moreover, solid preparation will allow the advocate to deal more easily and effectively even with
this unexpected ten percent. One can have far
greater confidence in following one's instincts
when those instincts have been educated and informed by solid preparation.

There are two facets of oral argument for
which the advocate must be prepared: the more
or less formal presentation and, usually far more
important, the responsiveness to the concerns of
the court. Both require meticulous planning and
preparation. Although the total time that an advocate will have for his presentation is determined in advance, it is usually difficult to predict
how much of that time will be taken up by questions and comments from the bench. Consequently, the lawyer's preparation of the formal
argument must be tailored to accommodate the
time constraints imposed on the spot. One method of dealing with this problem is to prepare
three different arguments: (1) a full argument

which assumes few or no questions from the bench and is designed to use the time allotted the advocate's position, (2) an intermediate argument, and (3) a short-form argument, which assumes a very active bench. Obviously, the first of these arguments is the most fully developed and will include not merely the main points that the advocate wishes to make but also the development of those points and whatever detail the advocate believes will prove helpful to her cause. By contrast, the last of these will include only those points that the advocate believes to be essential to her case.

As if this were not difficult enough, the reactions of the court may change during the course of the advocate's presentation. Thus, a court that is very active at the commencement of an advocate's presentation may become quiescent as the advocate continues; conversely, a court which begins passively may become increasingly active throughout the advocate's presentation. And, of course, the bench may shift from activity to passivity several times during the course of the presentation. Consequently, what is required is the flexibility to shift from one form of argument to another, often several times within the presentation.

Perhaps the best way to deal with this difficulty is by preparing the standard outline of a full argument with appropriate major and subsidiary points clearly delineated. A thorough familiarity with the outline should enable the advocate to move from major headings to sub-headings to details and back with some degree of facility. Many advocates find it helpful to use inks of different colors for the various levels or sections of argument so that a glance at the outline is sufficient. Of course, it is crucial for the advocate to rehearse this presentation several times in order both to gain the requisite facility and to obtain the sense of timing for the argument.

In addition to the need to be able to shift from one level of an argument to another is the need to be able to shift from one point of the argument to another. This need may arise either from the expressed wishes of the bench directing the advocate to address or abandon a particular point—a command which should always be obeyed (see Section 8–2)—or from the advocate's intuitive sense that a particular point or line of argument is either not necessary to advance because the court accepts it as established or is counterproductive to the advocate's position as a whole because the court finds it so clearly untenable that one is unlikely ever to persuade the court of the contrary.

The ability to "read" the court while in the midst of argument is an important skill for the successful advocate. Equally important, however, is being prepared to act upon the conclusions one draws as a result of this awareness. Thus, the advocate must be sufficiently familiar with the argument to be able to abandon a section of it and to move smoothly to the development of other points that can be pursued with greater profit. Finally, rehearsals also provide the advocate with an intimate familiarity with the layout of the argument so that, in the heat of combat, she can tell relatively quickly and easily what has been covered and what yet remains.

It should be noted that preparation even for the formal part of one's argument does not require, and in fact should not include, memorization. The job of the advocate is to persuade and few are persuaded by being read to or talked at by rote (see Section 8–3). Here, too, preparing the formal presentation in outline form rather than word for word should prove helpful.

Preparing for questions is best accomplished with the assistance of others. It is probably a good idea for the advocate preparing for oral argument to become a pest to colleagues, friends and family; that is, to prevail upon anyone who will accommodate her to listen to either the entire argument or parts of it and to inundate her with whatever questions they can think of. It often happens that after living with the case for an extended period, the lawyer develops a particular view or approach that may blind her to concerns that become apparent only from a different vantage point. Consequently, it is of some importance to present the argument to others who have some knowledge of the case but not the advocate's intensive immersion in it.

The advocate must be prepared for questions that range from the very sophisticated to the most basic. Thus, one should present her argument to colleagues who are expert in the particular field in which the case arises but should also present the case to those who know little about it. In other words, the argument should be comprehensible to the unsophisticated and ill-prepared judge as well as to the judge who is both very sophisticated and very well prepared on the particular issue. It is through this constant questioning from a variety of sources that one gains the confidence necessary to embark on an oral argument with knowledge that one can handle whatever comes.

After repeated performances before a number of different audiences, the advocate generally will be able to predict a number of particular questions or concerns likely to arise at the actual argument. Preparation for such questions should be very much like the preparation for the advocate's formal presentation; that is, the advocate ought to prepare vignettes of colloquy—bits and pieces of anticipated questions and answers—that can be used as the occasion requires.

In those instances in which a presentation is to be shared between two advocates, it is also important for each to be familiar with the other's argument. If a question should be asked with respect to a matter for which one's colleague is primarily responsible, it does not do to respond with, "My colleague will address that issue." Some cogent response is required and the only way to produce it is through thorough preparation of all facets of the argument.

It will sometimes happen during the course of an oral argument, especially with an active bench, that one question will lead to another question and that to yet another. By this second or third generation of questions the advocate may be taken rather far afield from her prepared presentation. And for this, too, one must be prepared. As we shall see, there are techniques by which one can return to matters more centrally concerned with one's argument; nonetheless, at least ideally, the advocate should be prepared to respond to two or three generations of questions beyond the immediate argument.

Finally, there is the less formal preparation whose aim is simply to acquire an intimate familiarity with all three aspects of the case: the record, the authorities and the advocate's argument based upon them. It requires that the advocate be so intimately acquainted with her position, the record and the points to be made that she can move from question to argument and back to next question without appearing flustered, and even more important, without destroying the logical flow and oratorical thrust of the argument.

There are few things worse in oral argument than to be found ignorant of the record or misstating it. The only way to avoid such a predicament is by a thorough mastery of everything in the record that might possibly be relevant to the argument. It is not sufficient to rely on a precis of the record prepared by another. There is simply no substitute for individual study of the proceedings already had in the case. (If more than one advocate is to participate in the argument, the game of "record trivia" played during spare moments can be a less oppressive aid to accomplishing the intimacy with the record that is essential.) Moreover, it is not sufficient merely to know the facts contained in the record cold; it is also necessary to be familiar with the physical layout of the record: to be able to put one's finger on a particular bit of testimony or a particular exhibit with a minimum of fuss. Tab indexing can be of some assistance in achieving this goal, but it cannot replace a thorough familiarity with the physical record.

A similar level of preparation is necessary with respect to the authorities upon which the advocate intends to rely. It is not sufficient to know only the proposition for which one intends to use a particular case. At least with respect to those few (and they should be few) cases that are to form the centerpiece of one's authority, the facts, procedural context and reasoning of the deciding court, as well as the underlying policies to be furthered by the decision must become second nature to the advocate. There is no guaranteeing that the court will passively accept the advocate's position with respect to any case upon which she relies. Thus, one must be prepared to deal with apparent distinctions in those cases suggested by the bench. The only way to do so is through the hard work necessary to become an authority on one's authority. (It should go without saying that the subsequent history of the cases upon which one relies must be verified, as must subsequent amendments to statutes, rules or regulations and any other developments in the field or with respect to the relevant issue. It is mortifying to be advised by the bench at oral argument that the case upon which one has placed principal reliance has been overruled, or worse, reversed on appeal.)

Finally, having become totally immersed in the record and the authorities, the advocate must also know the relationships between the various points in her argument and the way one part of the argument depends upon and fits into the other parts and the way in which each of these parts is related to the central theme upon which the argument rests. Equally important, the advocate must know, virtually instinctively, how all of this relates to everything in the record, where record support is to be found and so forth. Perhaps the best way of achieving this intimate familiarity with the structure and components of one's case is to organize and reorganize one's presentation in order to be able to get from one point of the argument to any other with a minimum of distraction. Here again, outlines can be extraordinarily helpful.

As we shall discuss in greater detail later (Section 8–11), the theme of the advocate's presentation plays a vital role in this ability to move about within the argument and from questions to the argument. Because everything in the advocate's presentation is related to the theme, a return to that theme will allow a connection to any substantial point elsewhere in the argument.

As can be seen from the foregoing, adequate preparation for fifteen or thirty minutes of oral argument is an extraordinarily difficult and time-consuming chore. One must recognize that something on the order of three-quarters of one's preparation for oral argument will not be put to any apparent use. Of course until it is too late, it is impossible to know which one-quarter will be necessary.

§ 8–2. Formalities

The formal requirements of oral argument vary in detail from court to court but remain essentially similar. One should of course be dressed appropriately: dark suits and ties for men and similarly conservative attire for women. That is, one's mode of dress ought to reflect the dignity of the occasion and project the respect the advocate ought to have for the tribunal before whom she is appearing.

The advocate should also find out before the time scheduled for her argument what the practice of the court is with respect to the identification of the advocate and her position and should, of course, follow that practice. Typically, the advocate upon first reaching the lectern, addresses the bench as follows: "May it please the court." This incantation is followed by an introduction: "I am . . . and I represent the petitioner (or respondent) ABC Corporation."

If the argument is to be divided, the court should be introduced to the advocate's colleague and should be told which advocate will argue what points. (Although in practice it is generally unwise to split an argument among several counsel, it is almost invariably the practice in law school moot court competitions.) Failure to identify the issues to be argued by each advocate is likely to result in questioning from the bench to advocate A on issues for which advocate B is better prepared. Despite even an explicit statement dividing the responsibilities of the advocates, the bench may not respect the division of labor, although advising the court of the assignment of each advocate does tend to minimize questions "off issue." Consequently, each advocate ought to be prepared on the entire case (see Section 8–1); though, usually, one will be somewhat better prepared on those issues for which she has assumed primary responsibility.

At the conclusion of one's presentation, the court should be thanked for its attention. This holds true regardless of how roughly the advocate may have been handled. When one's time has expired the court should be advised that that is the case. The court may sometimes be willing to grant additional time—at least enough to complete the point under discussion—but the advocate ought not exceed her allotted time without a clear invitation from the court that she do so.

Finally, the advocate must never address the bench from a seated position. Even for something as simple as responding to the bench's inquiry, "Is counsel prepared to proceed?" the advocate should rise before saying "yes." It is in such small ways that the advocate makes plain to the bench that she is aware of the deference and respect due the court.

This attitude of respect must always be maintained during the course of one's own argument and even during the presentation of one's adversary. So, for example, one ought not converse with one's colleague during her adversary's presentation. It is important to note, however, that the appropriate attitude is one of respect but not one of groveling. Thus, it is entirely appropriate, should the occasion demand it, to disagree with the bench. It is never appropriate, however, to treat the bench condescendingly or flippantly or disrespectfully. That the advocate may know more about the case or even about the law than does the judge, that the judge displays her ignorance, even her ineptitude, is no excuse for the advocate to exhibit anything less than responsible professional behavior. Her job is not to show the judge how dumb she is or how smart the advocate; it is to persuade her of the justness of the client's cause. Again, however, this does not require obsequiousness. An attitude of respectful intellectual equality strikes the right note.

Under no circumstances ought the advocate to interrupt the court. The temptation to do so is sometimes almost overwhelming. Resist it! The advocate has a limited amount of time in which to make her position clear. The judge may ask a question which takes ten minutes to articulate, though the advocate believes she knows the thrust of the question within the first ten seconds. Nonetheless the judge must be permitted to ask her question in her own time. The advocate must simply attend quietly, standing at the lectern and looking attentive. The advocate must train herself so that when a judge begins a question or looks as if she is about to ask a question, the advocate pauses instantly. There is a natural temptation to attempt to complete one's thought despite interruptions from the bench. The court is entitled to interrupt the attorney; the attorney is not entitled to interrupt the court. After all, it is the advocate who must persuade the bench, not vice versa. Consequently, she must be alert to their concerns; they need not be alert to hers.

Thus, if directed to address or abandon a particular point or line of argument, the advocate must do so. The points that the advocate had planned to make are less important than those the court wishes to hear. It is the court that has the responsibility of deciding. That is not to say, of course, that the advocate may not so develop her presentation as to make those arguments considered vital in a later context in which she has been able to demonstrate their importance.

To say that one should follow instructions given by the court is not to say that one should request such instruction. The advocate ought never voluntarily surrender control of the argument. Thus, for example, asking the court if it wishes to hear the facts is inappropriate; if the court is familiar with the facts and does not wish them formally presented, it is the court's place so to advise the advocate; it is not her place to ask. In addition to surrendering control, the initiation of questions on the part of the advocate may make for awkwardness in the argument. First of all, when a question is put by the advocate to a multi-judge panel, some one of the judges must take the responsibility of responding, perhaps in a way with which her colleagues would disagree. Thus, the court is made to feel uncomfortable. If, on the other hand, no member of the panel is willing to assume the responsibility of answering, the resulting silence is likely to be uncomfortable for those on both sides of the bench.

Finally, and perhaps most important, questions initiated by the advocate to the court are simply inappropriate. Such questions can be of only three kinds: requests for information, requests for instructions or challenges. An example of the first might be presented when a member of the panel asks about the effect of a particular decision with which the advocate may be unfamiliar. The appropriate response in such a situation is simply to admit one's ignorance of the case in question. Yet some advocates will ask the court to describe the case—in effect, to prepare them for their argument while it is going on. When the advocate admits her ignorance, the irritation the court may feel at her lack of preparation is tempered by their appreciation for her candor. When the advocate asks the court to provide the information she should already have had, the court's resentment at her ignorance is likely to be magnified by their irritation at her presumptuousness.

Requests for instructions, as we have already seen, mark a surrender of control. The inappropriateness of challenging the court, one might hope, requires no discussion. The only kind of question that can appropriately be addressed to the court is one seeking clarification of something said or requested by the court itself which is not entirely clear to the advocate.

Typically, one of the oral advocate's great enemies is time—more precisely, lack of time. The advocate has fifteen minutes, thirty minutes, an hour, to explain to the bench what the case is about, invoke and analyze the relevant authorities and demonstrate how those authorities support her position. There is never enough time.

On rare occasions, however (very rare), the miraculous may happen. The bench has not challenged the positions advanced or the advocate has so concisely and cogently stated the case that at the conclusion of her argument there is some time remaining. The advocate has run through every point in her outline, has fully developed them and is satisfied that the court has followed and understood; there is nothing remaining to be said. The best course for the advocate in that position is to thank the court, shut up and sit down. The urge to fill whatever time remains by repeating what has been said or, worse, by breaking new and untried ground is often overwhelming. It should be resisted. It never helps and almost always damages what may otherwise have been a solid performance. The court will not hold it against an advocate that she has completed her presentation in less than the allotted time. Indeed, the bench is likely to be grateful.

§ 8–3. Style

As noted in the previous section, the demeanor of the advocate toward the bench should evidence a respectful deference not a cowering obsequiousness. But formality should not be taken to the point of presenting a lecture to an audience. Persuasive argument is colloquy more than soliloquy. The ideal form is one in which the advocate converses with the court not one in which the advocate talks at the court. One of the aims of the exercise is to engage the court. And spontaneity, or the appearance of spontaneity, is a great help in accomplishing this.

Of course, as we have noted (Section 8–1), much careful preparation and planning is necessary to achieve spontaneity. To attempt to deliver an oral argument off the cuff is to court disaster. The rambling or overly conversational style that might be suitable for a discussion among law students over a keg of beer will win no points in the appellate courtroom. Similarly, attempts at humor are misplaced; unless perhaps one has achieved the rare distinction of a statesman of the law (there are few under 75 and not many more over that age), it is simply inappropriate to joke with the court. That is not to say that one should appear stiff and solemn. It has been suggested that Thomas Dewey lost the presidency in part because of the apparent cogency of Alice Roosevelt Longworth's crack that he was like the groom atop the wedding cake. If a member of the bench makes a joke—or what she believes to be a joke—it is perfectly permissible, even desirable, to share in the humor. The advocate, however, ought not initiate the witticisms nor attempt to engage in one-upsmanship. Thus, the proper attitude is neither too stiffly formal nor too casually relaxed.

It should be plain from the foregoing that reading to the bench from a prepared text is not likely to be the most successful method of presenting one's case. There are a number of reasons that one should rarely read anything in oral argument and never read much. First, if the advocate is to convince the court of the validity of her position, she must appear to believe in it herself. That is not to say, of course, that the advocate should express a personal opinion—or worse an emotional commitment—in her case; rather, it is to say that one ought to present an image or impression of belief in the validity of one's position and not appear to be going through the motions of advocacy simply because that is one's job. Reading from a script rarely can convey that impression of belief; it is simply too mechanical.

Moreover, while reading, it is almost impossible to maintain the eye contact with the members of the bench that is essential to persuasion. That sheet of paper between advocate and court operates as a brick wall. Additionally, the lack of eye contact tends to dehumanize all participants. One might just as well mail in a tape recording. One person can persuade another person; machines can neither persuade nor be persuaded. To the extent, therefore, that the advocate behaves as a machine or as if the members of the court were, she loses persuasive force.

Yet an additional problem with reading one's argument to the court is the necessity for shifting—usually with accompanying (and distracting) sound effects—various sheets of paper upon which the argument is recorded; and if, perish forfend, a question is asked, the reshuffling of those papers in an attempt to find the answer that must be there someplace compounds the distraction.

Finally, and perhaps most important, the presentation that is read tends to discourage questions. The most important parts of oral argument are the opportunities presented to the advocate to discover and resolve the doubts and difficulties that members of the court may entertain with respect to her position. Anything that hampers that process is to be avoided like the plague.

There is one exception—modification might be a better word—to the rule that says do not read to the court. If the case turns upon specific language (of statute, contract, will, regulation or so forth) that language should be read (or memorized and repeated) so that the precise terminology to be interpreted or applied is placed before the court. It is a good idea to note for the court where in the brief or its appendix the particular provision is to be found, so that they can follow with eye as well as ear, and so that the court can refer to it throughout the argument. This is usually done by first petitioner early in her argument. Occasionally, a particularly pithy quotation, especially from an admired judge, may prove helpful. In general, however, the use of quotations, unless they appear to be spontaneous, creates an artificial ambience. Quotations should be kept short and, if short, need not be read.

As bad as the written and read argument is the memorized and recited one. The argument committed to memory and spoken by rote has many of the same drawbacks as that committed to paper. Although it permits eye contact, it tends to be mechanical, lifeless and, for those reasons, unconvincing. It too discourages questions and militates against smooth transitions between the responses to any questions that may be asked and the advocate's return to her argument.

Perhaps one of the reasons for the written or memorized argument is the advocate's fear that there will come a time when, for a moment or two, she will need to think about what she wishes to say with the result that the courtroom will be silent; silence—any silence—being regarded as an enemy worse than death. Yet silence, constructively used, can be an extraordinarily effective device. Moreover, the silence that is likely to result from losing one's place in a set piece is the least likely to be effective. It is the silence of panic. Because we are so used to the sound of the human voice, especially in our appellate courts, silence is exceptional and, like most exceptional things, commands attention because of it. So, for example, an inattentive bench, one whose members are reading, or passing notes, can be virtually compelled to attend the advocate by the simple device of remaining silent. The absence of sound will attract the court's attention. One must be cautious, however, not to appear irritated by the court's lack of attentiveness.

The period of silence—the strategic pause—should be just long enough to attract the attention of the court. Similarly, it should be followed by the statement of a proposition of major importance to the advocate's position. Having attracted the court's attention, one ought not to squander it on unimportant details. Even shorter periods of silence can be put to effective use as devices of emphasis and pace. It is often, for example, quite effective to pause briefly at the conclusion of a judge's question, as if considering it before beginning one's answer. It suggests to the inquiring judge that the advocate believes the question sufficiently profound as to require reflection. And this is true although the question and answer may be entirely obvious and the advocate may have anticipated that very question and fully rehearsed the response she intends to make. An immediate response, without even a flicker of hesitation, may show the court how well the advocate could anticipate the question but may not be as convincing as the apparently more thoughtful reply.

An additional drawback to the memorized, and especially to the read, argument is that the voice of the speaker tends to drop in volume as she continues. An argument which cannot be heard cannot convince. Indeed, this is a danger even for the advocate who speaks only from notes or outline. It is critical that one retain an awareness of the volume at which one is speaking. Ideally, the advocate should know the courtroom —its size and acoustical properties—before the argument. One must be wary of practicing in a small office an argument which is to be given in a large courtroom.

Finally, the read or memorized argument tends to be presented in a monotone which further deadens whatever emotional appeal the argument might otherwise possess. Such qualities as emphasis and cadence are to oral argument what punctuation is to the written brief: They not only assist in the meaningful transmission of one's message but also provide a rhythm helpful to sustaining the interest of one's audience. A well-modulated and controlled voice is one of the most powerful assets of an effective advocate. This is not to say, of course, that the advocate should seek to persuade the court through an appeal to the emotion. Although every case, no matter how apparently dry or technical, has an emotional aspect which should not be neglected, the advocate should be wary indeed of presenting too aggressively emotional a case. (If there is any difference at all in the advice to be given male and female advocates, it is to emphasize for females this chariness about the appearance of emotionalism—not because women are more likely to commit this error, but because the appearance of a strong emotional component in a woman's presentation may encourage the unreconstructed judge to discount the merits of her argument. Thus, on this issue it is probably better

for female advocates to err on the side of restraint.)

Thus, for example, it is not good practice to
personalize the argument one is advancing;
phrases of personal belief or feeling should be
avoided. An argument couched in terms of "I
think," "I believe," "I feel" is inherently weaker
than the same argument made without the personalized introduction. Avoid the first person
pronouns. A corollary of this suggestion: Do not
—ever—advance personal attacks on your adversary, her client or the court below.

But to say that one's argument ought not be
personalized is not to say that one's case should
be treated as if all that were at stake were neutral principles or legal doctrine. Although true
of some cases more than others, all arguments
benefit if the court can be brought to an appreciation of the events giving rise to the litigation
in terms of the persons affected and of the consequences of decisional alternatives in the same
terms. Persons in this context may include institutional parties as well. Thus, in a most subtle
way, the advocate must suggest a duel between
the white hats and the black hats. It cannot be
overemphasized, however, that this must be done
with great care and circumspection. Little is
likely to stir the resentment of a bench more
than being addressed as one would address a jury.

Just as delivering a memorized or written out argument destroys the persuasive force of one's position, so too does the argument throughout which the advocate is constantly shuffling papers, notes, bits of the record, case or statutory authority. Such physical movement is not merely annoying to the court but also tends to distract attention from the content of the argument. Few of us are sufficiently confident to present an unmemorized argument without notes or references of some kind; nor is it necessary or advisable to do so. The notes to which the advocate refers, however, should be available without a search that consumes time and patience and produces irritation. Ideally, it should not be necessary even to turn a page. A glance at the lectern should be enough to call to the advocate's mind the step in the argument she wishes next to advance. Nor is it especially difficult to achieve this ideal. It will be recalled that we are not here speaking of a full argument written out with all transitional phrases and verbal flourishes. We are speaking rather of an outline, even if a rather complete one. One device often used is the legal size manila file folder. Such a folder is unobtrusive and neat when carried to the lectern; yet, when opened, it provides a surface of approximately seventeen by fourteen inches. And this using only one full side of the opened folder. Surely, the outline—no matter how complete—of a fifteen minute argument should be capable of reproduction over an area of 240 square inches. And this is especially true if one is as familiar as one should be not merely with the argument to be made but also with the physical layout of its appearance on the note card.

Similarly, it should not be necessary to fumble with the record to find bits and pieces that the advocate would like to use or about which the court has inquired. In addition to one's intellectual or analytic familiarity with the record, the advocate should be familiar with it physically as well. She should know where in the record various things appear. It is almost always helpful— and if the record is a long one, essential—to be able to find, with a minimum of fuss, just what is being sought. Similar familiarity is necessary with respect to one's own brief and the brief of one's adversary. Similarly, if it is anticipated that resort to specific other material is desirable (*e.g.*, the precise language of a statute, a late-breaking decision), these too should be accessible to the advocate at the lectern and with minimal distraction from the content of the argument. Many advocates use a loose-leaf notebook into which has been bound all of the materials which may be needed in the course of the argument, all properly indexed and tabbed for easy and efficient access. In addition to permitting the court to attend the content of one's argument without distraction, the appearance of workmanlike efficiency and control helps to create an atmosphere of craftsmanship and dependability.

One final note on style: No effective advocate attempts to portray a role in which she is uncomfortable. Most of us cannot capture the minds of others through the sheer drama and intensity of our own voice or performance. Although one can —and often should—moderate a particular style of speech, appearance or gesture to make one's total presentation more effective, one should not —probably cannot successfully—pretend to a style at odds with one's basic personality. All that is likely to be accomplished is that the advocate will appear phony, dishonest, insincere, and thus will cast doubt on her argument itself.

Thus, one whose basic personality is ebullient and who gesticulates and perambulates while speaking will find it necessary to curb the more grandiose gestures and, in general, to calm down. But to attempt to affect an icy calm is almost sure to result in disaster. Similarly, the calm, staid, soft-spoken advocate who resorts to histrionics out of fear of boring her audience is not likely to be successful. This is, of course, not to say that one should take no steps designed to improve one's performance or appearance at the lectern; it is only to suggest that ultimately you are what you are and cannot be what you are not.

Perhaps the most frequent masquerade is the advocate's attempt to appear more learned, high-toned or intellectually gifted. (This may also be part of the reason for the written or memorized argument.) It is bad enough to use apparently endless sentences made up of polysyllabic words in a brief where the reader can look back if necessary to remind herself who is doing what by the time she finds out to whom what is being done. In oral argument such abstruseness is unforgivable. The advice given in the previous chapter—short sentences, short words—applies in spades to the oral argument. And it applies with yet more emphasis to those—most of us—for whom the high falutin' mode of speech is not our natural way of expressing ourselves.

§ 8–4. First Petitioner

Despite their obvious similarities, each position in an oral argument presents difficulties and opportunities that differ in some respects from the other three positions. First petitioner has the opportunity to set the stage and as a result the tone for all that will follow. It is her job to introduce herself and her colleague, to advise the court of the nature of the case before it and, perhaps most important, to state the facts upon which the legal dispute is based. Ideally these facts should be stated in such a way that, at their conclusion, the justice of petitioner's cause is plainly apparent.

First petitioner should begin by introducing herself and her colleague and identifying the party on whose behalf she speaks. Thus, "I am Joan Marshall and with my colleague, Betsy Ross, represent the petitioner in this action, the ABC Corporation." This should be followed by a brief statement of the kind of case presented and the route by which it came to the appellate court: "This is a civil antitrust case, here on certiorari to the Fourteenth Circuit which affirmed a judgment for the defendant." The third point first petitioner must make is, at least in broad terms, the nature of the issue the appellate court is called upon to decide: "It presents the question whether . . ."

Only after this has been done—the context set —should petitioner proceed to state the facts of the case. The facts should be stated in such a way as to engage the interest of the court. Yet they must not be over-dramatized. Additionally, one ought not make the statement of facts so detailed as to include irrelevant items, nor so general as to neglect those facts which might influence the decision. It must be kept in mind that the great enemy of the oral advocate is time. Thus, intricate factual detail not necessary to the development of the argument should be omitted unless

—and it is an important unless—to do so would give an unfairly distorted view of the case. Determining the appropriate degree of generality and detail is one of the skills which go into making the art of oral argument.

As a general rule (it should be emphasized that this is merely a guideline), first petitioner should be ready to start the argument (*i.e.*, should be finished with the introduction and statement of facts) after three or three and a half minutes. Thus, if the argument itself had been evenly divided in terms of the time allotted—fifteen minutes per advocate—first petitioner will have only eleven and a half or twelve minutes to make her presentation. Consequently, the time necessary for introduction and statement of facts must be considered in the division of time among participants; first petitioner should either have a shorter argument to make or be given correspondingly more time to make it. One way of equalizing the time for argument itself is to subtract any time reserved for rebuttal from second petitioner's argument. This problem of dividing time obviously will depend largely upon the nature of the case to be presented, the organization of the argument and the time needed for each issue. The analytic integrity of the argument should never be sacrificed for the sake of equalizing the time for its presentation.

Finally, first petitioner, unlike the advocates in the other positions, must be prepared with an extra level of argument. Although all the advocates must be prepared to argue to a bench that may fill her time with questions or may sit like statues permitting the advocate to develop the entire argument in all its exquisite detail, only first petitioner must contend not only with the range of time resulting from differences in the activity of the bench, but must also be prepared for a bench that waives the statement of facts. So, if first petitioner is allotted fifteen minutes for her presentation and has set aside three minutes for the facts, it should become obvious that an extra few minutes of argument time will be available should the bench say, "We're familiar with the facts counselor. Proceed with your argument." Thus, first petitioner must be prepared not only with the three levels of argument previously discussed (see Section 8–1) but with an additional level to be used in the event the facts need not be stated.

§ 8–5. Second Petitioner

There are three points to be made with respect to second petitioner's argument. Ordinarily, second petitioner will be asked more questions by the bench than was first petitioner. It usually takes the bench a few minutes to get warmed up, either to recall enough about the case or to learn enough about it to be able to formulate its questions. Some measure of first petitioner's time will already have expired by the time the court begins its questioning. Again, it is important to note that this is certainly not invariably the case. Nonetheless it happens with sufficient frequency to be notable. Consequently, second petitioner is more likely to get questions not only with respect to her own segment of the argument, but also with respect to her colleague's than is first petitioner. It is even more important therefore for second petitioner to be familiar with the entire case than it is for first petitioner. Second petitioner presents the last opportunity for the court to inquire about any aspect of petitioner's case.

This leads to the second point to be made about the second petitioner's argument. Second petitioner must be alert to the concerns of the bench during her colleague's presentation. Because she will speak last for her side it is up to second petitioner to alleviate any concerns that the court may have with respect to any aspect of the case, including those concerns made evident and not satisfactorily resolved during the first argument. Thus, second petitioner ought not use the time during first petitioner's argument to review her own presentation. Rather, that time should be spent in close concentration on the interaction between advocate and bench.

Finally, as first petitioner has the opportunity to set the stage for what is to follow, it is the responsibility of second petitioner to leave the court with the appropriate perspective or perception. Petitioner's position must be summed up in a way that incorporates both segments of the argument, states petitioner's theme of the case and adumbrates the justice of petitioner's cause. In the ideal world this summing up will be done in two or three sentences and will conclude precisely as petitioner's time expires, leaving second petitioner only enough time to say, "Thank you, your Honors."

§ 8–6. First Respondent

In at last one respect respondents have an easier time of it than petitioners. Respondents will have had the time of petitioner's argument during which to observe the bench in action. Careful attention to the petitioner's argument and the court's verbal and non-verbal responses to it can provide important and useful information to respondents. Obviously then, respondents ought not use the time in which petitioner is making the argument to prepare or review their own arguments one last time. Rather, respondents should pay close attention to what is transpiring during petitioner's argument. Of special significance are questions put by the bench to which the petitioner has responded inadequately or the concerns of the bench which petitioner does not appear to have satisfied. A respondent who answers those questions or addresses those concerns is that much ahead of the game.

This advantage is balanced to some extent by the fact that a respondent sometimes needs to be more flexible, more prepared to deviate from her prepared argument, in order to take advantage of the additional information provided her during petitioner's argument. These concerns should of course be addressed in a way that integrates the responses smoothly into the argument for the respondent. If respondent has adequately prepared, most of these concerns will be dealt with during the course of the argument. What respondent must do to take advantage of whatever new information is gained during petitioner's argument is to highlight this material or perhaps to expand it at the sacrifice of other points with which the bench seems less concerned. So, for example, it would not be inappropriate for respondent, when about to discuss an issue with which some member of the court has expressed concern during petitioner's argument to say, "As Judge X has remarked . . ." This demonstrates to the court the advocate's concern that the bench be satisfied with all aspects of the case, while at the same time calling attention to the weaknesses in the opponent's case and guaranteeing the attention of at least that judge who questioned petitioners.

Just as first petitioner is responsible for setting the stage, so too first respondent must introduce herself and her colleague and alert the bench to the theme of respondent's position. It is generally the task of first respondent to move the court from the vantage point that petitioner has attempted to establish to one with a very different perspective. First respondent must set the context for respondent's entire argument.

This chore is made all the more difficult by the fact that, at least typically, it is first respondent who is likely to face the bench at its most active point. During first petitioner's argument the bench will often tend to be cold, familiarizing or re-familiarizing themselves with the case. Generally the fewest questions will be asked during first petitioner's argument. By the time second petitioner begins her argument the bench is beginning to warm up, but because the issue has changed the bench may still be searching for a handle on the case. By the time first respondent rises, however, the court will have become familiar with the case generally and with the issues with which first respondent is to deal. Hence, at this point the court feels comfortable enough and familiar enough with what is going on to be quite active. This is an additional reason for first respondent to be prepared to move from point to point in her argument with a good deal of flexibility. Achieving this flexibility without appearing to be choppy or disintegrated is a difficult skill to acquire—but one that is of extreme importance and value.

§ 8–7. Second Respondent

Because of the often high level of activity of the court during first respondent's argument, it may become necessary for second respondent, in addition to explicating the issues for which she is primarily responsible, to cover at least some of the ground first respondent may not have been permitted to reach. Second respondent is in the unenviable position of having the last opportunity for her side to address the bench. As a consequence, it is up to her to fill in any gaps, resolve any lingering concerns that the bench may have with respect to respondent's case—this in addition to presenting her own argument.

Finally, it is up to second respondent to summarize for the bench respondent's entire case and to leave the court with the theme of that case firmly established. Second respondent more than any other position should strive to complete her argument with a relatively polished few sentences that accomplishes this end. She should be able to begin her conclusion from several different points in her argument when there remains only a minute or so of her allotted time.

§ 8-8. Rebuttal

Petitioners should always reserve a few minutes of rebuttal time. There are two schools of thought on the way this time should be used. Under the first view, petitioners should always use the time they have reserved. Under the second view, petitioners will rarely use this time. Proponents of the first view argue that the time permitted for oral argument is scarce and valuable and, consequently, not a moment of it should be wasted. They also argue that rebuttal time presents petitioners with the opportunity to leave the court with their position, rather than respondent's, uppermost in the court's mind. It is said that rebuttal should be used to emphasize and underscore petitioner's theme of the case and to summarize petitioner's argument once again.

Proponents of the second view take the position that time reserved for rebuttal should be used for rebuttal and that if respondents have said nothing that requires rebuttal, petitioners ought to waive the time they have reserved. The proponents of this view believe that as second respondent completes her argument, the bench is beginning to wind down. They are often at least psychologically tired. As a result, they may resent being forced to listen to a rehash of arguments petitioner has already made during her presentation in chief.

Whichever view one takes, rebuttal time should not be used merely to pick nits in respondent's presentation. Errors or misstatements which are inconsequential should not be the subject of a rebuttal argument. It is worth reiterating that the function of oral argument is not to demonstrate to the bench how bright or well prepared is the advocate, but rather how worthy of relief is the party on whose behalf the advocate appears. Thus, if respondents have misstated a major case —one of some real importance to the argument —that should be corrected on rebuttal. Similarly, if respondents have misstated important facts, that too should be corrected on rebuttal. Finally, and perhaps most important, if respondents have failed adequately to answer questions or concerns of the bench, petitioner should do so on rebuttal. Incidentally, it is probably a good idea to respond to the question from the bench, "Is there any rebuttal?" with the introductory clause, "Very briefly, your Honors"—and then to live up to that promise.

§ 8-9. Use of Authority

Not surprisingly, the use of authority in oral argument is different from its use in the brief. These differences reflect the larger differences between the two forms of argument. In the written brief authorities can be used with far more subtle refinement. Because the reader retains the ability to return to the advocate's analysis or exposition, elegant complex treatment is possible and often necessary.

Because, on the other hand, an oral argument presents only an immediate sensory experience for the court, what cannot be quickly grasped is certain to be lost. Even worse, the failure to grasp the advocate's intricate analysis of a particular point or case may be viewed by the court as a weakness in the advocate's position. Perhaps still worse, confusion on the part of the court may lead to a series of questions with respect to a relatively minor though conceptually difficult segment of the argument, the result of which may be to exhaust the advocate's limited time— time that obviously would have been far more effectively spent on the essential points of her position.

Thus, the first point to be made about the use of authority in oral argument is to keep it simple. If the use or application of a particular authority requires elaborate explanation, it is not likely to be effective in oral argument unless the particular authority is the keystone of the advocate's entire case. It is important to note that this is not to suggest that the principles or policies underlying a particular authority should not be used; they should to whatever extent they apply and are persuasive.

The other exception to an extended discussion of authority arises out of the necessity of distinguishing authority apparently on point and opposed to the position being advanced by the argument. Here it is crucial to convince the court that the statute or prior decision is not controlling or—still better—that when the principle or rationale of the authority is applied to the peculiar facts of this case, the authority itself requires (or at least suggests) a contrary result. Even in such a situation, however, it is likely that the better argument will not rest on an elaborate analysis of the particular authority but on its underlying policy basis or on the principles on which it rests. And, of course, if there are only one or two principal authorities, whether affirmative or negative, that form the linchpin of one's case, they must be analyzed. But, if this is so, most of the argument is likely to revolve about this center, so that the authorities are not being used as such but as the focal point of the advocate's entire presentation.

As important as avoiding authority that results in conceptual complexities unsuited to oral presentation, is avoiding the laundry list of authorities. It is not persuasive to "trash cite" in the brief; it is disastrous to do so in orals. There are two reasons for this. First, although it never hurts to have authority on one's side, it is rarely enough. To concentrate entirely on favorable authority at the cost of a presentation based on policy and principle is rarely successful.

The second reason to avoid a plenitude of authority in oral argument is the inability of the human—even the judicial—mind to retain a large number of concretes. It must be borne in mind that the court will rarely have the advocate's familiarity with the cases. More important, if the argument is otherwise well-fashioned, the advocate should be able to retain all the authorities in mind because of the pattern or context she has established and into which they fit. The court is unlikely to have the same advantage. The advocate is far better advised to establish the appropriate context for the court and leave the work of filling in the details and embellishing the outline with appropriate authority to the brief. Thus, unless the advocate can be sure that the court is thoroughly familiar with the case and with the doctrinal background against which it is to be decided, extensive discussion of previous decisions or other relevant authority is neither possible nor desirable in the short time available for oral argument. Far better to expose the jugular vein of the case and then attack it.

Finally, it is not unimportant to note that a litany of cases—some advocates even include the full citations—is boring. Almost always they must be read rather than spoken. Whatever interest the advocate may have piqued is likely to be rapidly dissipated by what sounds like an oral treatise, complete even to footnotes.

§ 8–10. Hot and Cold Benches

Perhaps the single greatest difference between the neophyte advocate and her more experienced colleague is reflected in their attitudes toward questions from the bench. The neophyte tends to dread them; the veteran is far more concerned with their absence. There is little worse for the veteran advocate than to be confronted with a silent bench—a bench that may or may not appear to listen to the advocate's presentation but that says nothing and does not change expression. Such benches are called cold benches, perhaps because the dead are cold.

A moment's reflection should reveal the difficulty presented the advocate by such a bench. The great advantage of oral argument is the opportunity to engage the mind and attention of the court, to be able to determine and to deal directly with those aspects of one's position found troublesome by the court. It is a great advantage to learn whether one's position has been understood, what portions of it need further clarification, what difficulties have not been dealt with adequately and to be able to attempt to cure the deficiencies and resolve the doubts. Yet it is only when the court talks back that this can be effectively undertaken. Thus, oral advocacy at its best is not a monologue by the advocate, but a dialogue with the court—a colloquy rather than a soliloquy.

It is far less important to her case that the advocate present each and every point she had intended to present in precisely the order she had intended, than it is that she respond to and resolve the doubts and concerns of those who will render a decision in the case. Thus, interruptions should not be resented as an interference, but welcomed as an opportunity.

As we have indicated earlier, there are predictable patterns of activity that hold true for most (though, of course, not all) benches. Typically, the beginning of petitioner's argument and the end of respondent's argument are the points at which courts tend to be most quiescent. It is important to recognize this for two reasons. First, and most important, almost all arguments rest upon a few fundamental propositions which must be established if the proponent is to prevail. Those propositions constitute the advocate's minimal argument. Whether the bench is lively or not, petitioner should attempt to make these points early; respondent, on the other hand, can afford to wait until somewhat later in her argument, should that appear helpful. Of course, respondent is likely to have a far better sense of the level of activity of the bench that she can anticipate, having observed its behavior toward petitioner. Yet even petitioner should have some notion based upon her knowledge of the members of the court or her observation of other arguments before the same panel.

Second, if the argument is to be shared among two advocates, one may be more comfortable with an active panel while the other prefers to present a more formal argument with fewer interruptions. If that is the case, it is a factor to be considered in determining the positions each advocate will argue. (It is the extraordinary case, however, in which this factor is determinative. Typically, the advocate most familiar with a particular branch of the case, as a result either of preparation for the particular case or of familiarity with the area of law, should argue that issue and its organizational position should depend upon the structure of the argument more than on the preference of the advocate.)

The ideal bench is, like Baby Bear's porridge, neither too hot nor too cold. They ask a number of questions which the advocate has anticipated and for which she has thoroughly prepared, though apparently spontaneous, answers. Yet the questions and comments from the bench are not so frequent nor so tangential as to break the flow of the argument or interfere with the advocate's ability to make and develop all the points she had intended to do. Unfortunately, like Baby Bear's porridge, such benches are the stuff of fairy tales. Far more typical are benches that are either too cold—providing little feedback to the advocate and inhibiting the engagement of minds so necessary to the process of persuasion—or too hot—asking so many or such tangential questions, making so many comments, arguing so among themselves, that the points necessary to the advocate's case are lost in the turmoil.

It is important, therefore, that the advocate develop techniques to assist her in controlling the bench's activity. Although the advocate should never appear to control the court, the best advocates in fact maintain a very high level of control over the argument and even over the bench; but they do so in a way that is entirely unobtrusive, always maintaining the proper attitude of deference and respect.

There are two aspects to this control: cooling off a too hot bench and warming up a dead one. The first step with respect to both, however, is the same. It is recognizing the problem and also recognizing that there are steps the advocate can take to alleviate it.

The hyperactive bench generates an energy and a tension that feeds on itself and makes the bench yet more active. Sure signs of this problem are colloquies among the members of the court leaving the advocate silent and alone at the lectern, consecutive questions with no hiatus in which the advocate can respond, questions leading to other questions roaming farther and farther afield from the issues of the case. Often one can observe the advocate caught up in this tension and completely surrendering her control of the argument to the bench.

What must be done, of course, is to defuse the tension, to reduce the energy. It is easier to take the necessary steps to accomplish this earlier rather than later. As we have noted repeatedly throughout this book, the power of inertia is the strongest power in the world. Thus, just as it is easier to stop an automobile traveling at five miles per hour than it is one travelling at thirty, it is generally easier to prevent judicial hyperactivity than it is to stop it after it has gained momentum. Here again there is some disadvantage to first petitioner—borne of ignorance. Most courts tend to be at their least active at the beginning of an advocate's presentation. Those advocates, therefore, who follow first petitioner, will have a much better notion, based upon their observation of the bench's behavior during first petitioner's argument, whether it is necessary to take steps early to cool down the argument. First petitioner, on the other hand, lacking this early warning signal, may have a more difficult time overcoming the inertia of an activity level well underway before the necessity to take steps to remedy the situation becomes apparent.

Assuming then that the advocate has determined that the bench is becoming hyperactive in a way that is likely to reduce the effectiveness of her presentation, what steps can she take to alleviate the problem? First and foremost in importance, and perhaps most difficult, is not to permit oneself to be stampeded into a corresponding level of tension and activity. As we have said, there is a tendency for such a situation to feed on itself, worsening and worsening throughout the argument. Consequently, the advocate must remain calm and must seek to defuse the tension already existing. Perhaps the most effective device for accomplishing this is to slow the pace of the proceedings. Thus, the advocate should speak more slowly, should take a moment longer to respond to questions, should pause more and for longer periods when speaking. The timing of these pauses is critical, however. They should always occur after the court has asked a question or made a comment and before the advocate addresses it or during the advocate's response. They should never be left to the conclusion of the advocate's statement. A pause at that point invites—almost demands from an active bench—another question. Thus, when completing her response to something said by the court, the advocate should continue on with her argument without pause.

Similarly, because the object is to reduce tension and activity, the advocate should lower her voice, reduce expressiveness and inflection, eliminate gestures. She should strive for a more relaxed posture or stance at the lectern. It must be emphasized, however, that these devices must be employed with the greatest subtlety. The changes in the advocate's demeanor should be hardly noticeable. It is all too easy to fall into a caricature of oneself by overdoing. Practice is necessary in order to achieve the sense of timing that will prevent overplaying.

Yet another manifestation of judicial heat is hostility. One or more members of the panel may seem to disagree with the advocate's position or attempt to test the limits of the principle she is advancing or question whether prior cases are inconsistent with the result she is seeking. If the advocate continues to press a hard line, the disagreement is likely to escalate into hostility. Perhaps the best way to short-circuit this destructive reaction is through the tactical concession. It is important not to respond with impatience or confrontation—a head to head conflict between judge and advocate can have only one outcome. Consequently, tactical retreat is sometimes necessary.

Of course, if the position with which a member of the panel disagrees is the heart of the advocate's case, she cannot concede it. Rarely, does this occur, however. More often the bench questions some matter that will not be determinative of the outcome. In such cases, the advocate should, at least, validate the question; that is, she should be able to appreciate the reasons underlying the concern, admit them, but then demonstrate the reasons that they do not apply to the case at bar. It is critical for the advocate in this position to know precisely what she may concede and what she can not concede without giving up her case. Validating the expressed concerns of the court is usually an effective method of cooling off judicial hostility before it can become destructive.

The problem of the "dead bench" presents yet greater obstacles to the advocate's ability to persuade; worse, the solution to the problems presented by the dead bench are harder to achieve and riskier to execute.

First, the problems. Some of these we have already touched upon: Dialogue is a more persuasive form of persuasion than monologue; judges' concerns about a case's weaknesses that remain unvoiced remain unaddressed. In addition to these, however, is the problem of determining the extent to which the bench must be educated with respect to the case. To some extent this is predictable. There are courts in which it is customary for the judges to gain their first (or nearly their first) exposure to the case through oral argument; there are courts in which it is custom-ary for the judges to be quite familiar with the briefs and the record before argument. In courts that follow either custom—or indeed any other with respect to level of preparation before argu-ment—the dead bench presents somewhat less of a problem. The advocate at least has some idea of what can be taken for granted and what must be established.

But there are courts that follow no particular custom. Worse, there are courts in which the level of preparation of various judges on the same panel differ dramatically. (Academic moot courts are often characterized by the grossest sorts of inconsistencies in the preparation the judges bring to oral argument.) And, if a bench is unresponsive, it becomes extraordinarily diffi-cult for the advocate to know at what level of preparation to pitch the argument.

Thus, it is important to develop techniques through which one can enliven the argument, wake up the court; for without communication from the court, effective communication to it be-comes problematic. Some of these techniques should be obvious; they are the reverse of those used to quiet the hyperactive bench. Thus, the advocate should become more animated; the vol-ume and expressiveness of her voice should in-crease; gestures should become more flamboyant. Again, however, great caution is necessary to avoid overdoing; these changes must be quite subtle and beneath the level of the court's consciousness.

One other device may help to stimulate an overly quiescent court: silence. The use of silence in this context, however, obviously is different from its use as a device to quiet the hyperactive bench. There, silence was used to lengthen the time in which a particular number of events occurred; it was used to slow the time during which a lot of things were happening. Here, it is used to create empty time; time in which nothing is happening. It is in this context that pausing after completing a response to some statement or question from the bench can be helpful. It provides the cushion of time that permits—encourages—another question. Two things are likely to follow from this use of silence: First, the bench will pay attention. If the judges have not been attending—have been writing letters or notes or even chatting among themselves—silence is virtually guaranteed to cause them to sit up and take notice. Second, and for this purpose more important, it is likely to cause at least one member of the court to say something to fill that awful void. It is then up to the advocate to take the ball and run with it, to try to create the inertial force that will keep the bench attentive and active.

Of course, this technique, like any other technique, will not always be successful. Yet little is lost by using it once or twice in an argument. It is surely simple enough to continue if the bench does not accept the invitation to participate extended by the advocate's silence. It remains only to develop the time sense that permits the advocate to judge the optimal point at which to terminate the period of silence to avoid the impression that she is halting because of some weakness in her argument or lack of ability to articulate her position. Finally, such silent periods as there are should be so placed as to create an impression of thoughtfulness rather than stumbling. In short, the point in the argument at which these silences appear must be carefully planned and their duration just as carefully controlled.

There is one final device sometimes used to awaken the quiescent court. It is, however, extremely dangerous, with the potential for doing far more harm than good. Consequently, it must be used with great care and is not recommended for the neophyte. It consists in stating a point so obviously outrageous that the court is not likely to allow it to pass unchallenged. Such statements must be prepared with the most exquisite care for they must be only apparently outrageous. The advocate must have an explanation ready to demonstrate that this appearance is a false one. The explanation must show not only why the proposition is ultimately correct but also that that very reason forms the basis of the advocate's position in the case. Ideally, the explanation is advanced in response to the anticipated challenge by the court. If no such challenge is forthcoming, however, the advocate must nonetheless proceed with the demonstration. The risk inheres in the very outrageousness of the original proposition for it may lead the court to discount much else of what the advocate has to say. It is the very opposite of what most advocates should strive for most of the time: understatement. Typically, overstating one's position or the support upon which it rests is likely to result in a loss of credibility that may be difficult to regain. Thus, this technique works in very few cases and can be used successfully by even fewer advocates. Where it does work, however, it is stunning.

§ 8–11. Questions

The appropriate way to deal with questions from the bench reflects the underlying purpose of oral argument: to make contact with the minds of the judges and to dispel any uncertainties and clarify any doubts about the correctness of the advocate's position. Thus, the cardinal rule for responding to questions is to answer them.

Never, ever evade!

Among the more grievous faults of which an advocate may be guilty, the failure to respond quickly, forthrightly and candidly stands close to the top of the list. This failure may take many forms. Among the most egregious is simply ignoring the question. As improbable as it may seem, advocates have been known to become so involved in their arguments that they do not hear or attend interruptions from the bench. Of course, not having heard the question, the advocate, not surprisingly, makes no attempt to respond, instead proceeding blithely on her way to a deserved oblivion. That the particular judge may have mumbled or spoken softly is no excuse. The lesson to be learned is that it is critical to remain sensitive to the court before whom one is arguing. Indeed, the better advocate will know a moment before it occurs that a member of the panel is about to interrupt. Telltale body language and especially eye movement often provide notice of a judge's intention to the advocate whose antennae are sensitive enough to receive it. The advocate must pay attention to the actions and reactions of the court as well as to her own presentation. This attention should minimize the danger of the unperceived question.

Assuming that a question has been asked and that the advocate has heard it, the next step is to be sure that the advocate's understanding of the content of the inquiry corresponds to that of the judge who initiated it. There is the story of the small boy who asked his mother, "Mommie, where did I come from?" The mother, being a progressive parent, explained to the child in great detail the process of human reproduction. At the conclusion the little boy responded, "I know all about that, but Mary said she came from New Jersey; where did I come from?" It is all too easy to believe that a judge is asking a far more sophisticated question than she is, in fact, asking. This is not to denigrate the intellectual capacity of our judges; but almost certainly the advocate will have so much more knowledge of the particular case than will the court that—like the boy and his mother—misunderstanding about the information being sought is not uncommon.

The failure to apprehend the question results in its not being answered. Like the little boy who did not find out whence he came, the judge who asked the question will remain dissatisfied, his concerns will not have been set at rest. Moreover, the response to the more sophisticated question that was not asked may lead to long explanatory digression that eats into the advocate's limited time with no corresponding value in persuasiveness.

A somewhat different problem may also arise from the same cause, the advocate's failure to apprehend the question asked because of her expectations of the kind of questions likely to be asked. In this other manifestation, the difficulty arises from the advocate's view of the court as her adversary. As a consequence, any question asked is expected to be and is viewed as a hostile question. (This problem is especially acute in law school moot court competitions, although it is by no means limited to academic exercises.) Frequently, of course, such a perception is far from the mark. Judges may well ask friendly questions— questions that allow the advocate to make a point that will support the inquiring judge's agreement with her or to support a position that may have been insufficiently developed. When the advocate erroneously responds to such a question as if it were a hostile challenge, she not only foregoes the opportunity presented by the question but also displays her lack of understanding of her position or her inattention to the bench or both.

There are two steps the advocate can take to minimize misunderstanding a judge's question, comment, remark or instruction. First and most obvious, the advocate must listen to the question. Despite its obviousness, it is astonishing how often advocates fail to follow this simple commandment. Frequently the advocate will be considering her response before the question is completed, thereby giving less than full attention to the end of the judge's communication. Sometimes she will be indulging her irritation at being interrupted. Perhaps it is merely that she has never learned the art of listening closely and carefully to what another is saying. Whatever the reasons, one of the major causes for misapprehending a judge's message is the failure to listen.

Even if one has listened carefully to the judge, however, it may be that the import of the message remains unclear. The question may be ambiguous; the judge may herself be unsure of precisely what is troubling her and hence be able only to approximate her concern. Perhaps the most useful device for clarifying such a question is to suggest the meaning the advocate believes the judge wished to convey and inquire as to whether the suggestion is an accurate one: "I want to be sure I understand your question. If you are asking .   .   ." This accomplishes several things. Of no small importance, it conveys to the court that the advocate is seriously concerned with the court's questions and wishes to deal with them forthrightly. Additionally, it serves to clarify precisely what the question is so that it can be answered without wasting precious time on factors of the case about which the court is not actually concerned.

Incidentally, the failure of communication with respect to the judge's initial question should not be laid at the judge's feet. It is far better for the advocate to accept responsibility for failing to receive the message than to blame the judge for a fault in transmission. Thus, "I'm not sure I understand the question," rather than "The question is not clear."

The practice of rephrasing questions from the court can provide an additional benefit. It permits the advocate to exert a significantly greater measure of control over the course of the argument. One must be cautious, however, in the use of this technique. It is not appropriate, nor is it helpful to the advocate's cause, for her to decide that she does not like the court's question, to rephrase it into one she prefers and then to answer the latter. Appellate judges are rarely so dense as to fail to realize that the advocate that behaves in this way is not being candid. Moreover, it leaves the question originally put unanswered.

If the technique is to be used, the rephrased question must include the crux of the concern evidenced by the original. The rephrasing should do no more than provide a somewhat different shading, either for purposes of clarification or to permit more of the advocate's argument to be included in her response or to permit the advocate to conclude her response in a way that more comfortably leads back to the point in the argument at which she plans to resume it. Thus, the rephrased question can serve as an organizational hinge for the advocate's argument.

It should also be noted that points made in response to questions are likely to be more effective than the same points made during the normal course of argument. This is certainly true with respect to the judge who asked the question and is probably true for the court as a whole. Thus, rephrasing a question may serve the additional function of allowing the advocate to make or develop a position that would in any event be a necessary part of her argument. (Indeed, truly polished and experienced advocates may sometimes so formulate a particular assertion or section of their arguments as to invite particular sorts of questions for which they, of course, have carefully prepared responses. The tip-off to such a ploy is the long pause following a statement that appears incomplete, incorrect or even outrageous. The purpose of the pause, of course, is to present the court the opportunity to ask the expected question.) It is often in this way that the thoroughly prepared analytic vignettes previously considered (Section 8–1) may make their way into the advocate's presentation.

As we said at the outset of this section, it is crucial to answer any question put by the court. The failure to do so—and to do so immediately—has three interconnected consequences, none desirable. First, the court may assume that the unanswered question exposes a weakness in the advocate's position with which she is incapable of dealing; second, the court may assume either that the advocate is inadequately prepared or lacking in candor; third, the attention of the court may be diverted from the substance of the adversary's argument to reflection on that unanswered question.

More common than ignoring questions from the bench, perhaps even more common than failing to listen and understand them, are two other faults in dealing with questions. The first involves the advocate so wedded to her own organization of the argument that it requires a crowbar to pry her loose. Such an advocate is likely to respond to the court's question with "I am coming to that" or "I shall answer your question in a few moments." At least the judge that asked the question, and probably other members of the bench, is likely to have her attention fixed on that question until it is answered and hence will give less attention to what the advocate has to say between the question and the answer. Worse, in the heat of oral argument the question may be forgotten or the advocate's time may expire before she has the opportunity to return to the question. In that event, not only does the court's concern remain unanswered, but the advocate has placed herself in the position of making a representation to the court and then failing to live up to it. Finally, the postponing response is too overt an attempt to control the court and is likely to be viewed—correctly—as a display of disrespect to the bench's dignity.

This problem of postponing one's answer to the court can become especially acute in cases in which two advocates are sharing an argument. It will sometimes happen that during the argument of the first advocate to speak for a particular position a judge will ask a question with which the second advocate is better prepared to deal. Attempting to put off the question until that time has all of the drawbacks of the sort of postponement already discussed and, in addition, may cause organizational difficulties for one's colleague, who may be confronted with that question immediately upon advancing to the lectern. Far better to respond to the question even if the response is followed by, "My colleague will address that matter in greater detail." Of course, as we have seen, such occurrences can be minimized—though not eliminated—by a careful delineation of responsibility in the first advocate's introduction.

The final and probably most frequent flaw in responding to questions occurs when the advocate appears to have answered the question when in fact she has not. This can happen for two reasons. Sometimes the advocate believes she has answered; sometimes the failure to answer is purposeful. Regardless of what prompted the flaw, it is deleterious to the argument. Typically, it occurs when the advocate's response to a question is a long involved explanation of a position that the advocate has never taken or of a point she has not made. At times it is an attempt to demonstrate why the question does not hurt the position being advanced or even why it (the question) is not relevant to the case. In any event, it seldom provides a direct response. And the court usually knows it. Even when not intended to be evasive it may appear so, perhaps causing the court to doubt the advocate's candor.

Fortunately the problem is relatively simple to solve. The advocate need only train herself to *first* respond with a clear expression of agreement or disagreement with the point of the question. Only *after* this clear "Yes" or "No" should any necessary explanation be advanced. The failure to do so may merely reflect the advocate's fear of taking a firm position without being certain of where that position may lead. The answer to such trepidation, however, is thorough preparation. If the advocate has thoroughly immersed herself in her case, she should be sufficiently confident of her instincts that even an unanticipated question can be responded to unambiguously—certainly after a brief pause to consider the import of the question and the consequences of various responses.

It is important to note that what we are speaking of here is the question addressing the position being advanced by the advocate. If the question concerns a matter of record fact or of the holding of an authority or other similar question of verifiable material, it is never sufficient to trust one's instincts. If the answer to the question is right or wrong and the advocate is unsure, it is essential to admit that fact. It is always professionally irresponsible to lie to the court. And let there be no mistake about this: pretending to a knowledge one does not possess is lying. Far better to admit candidly this gap in one's preparation and to volunteer to submit supplemental briefs or at least to investigate and advise the court (and, of course, one's adversary) on the matter later. In this way, at least, though the court may resent the advocate's lack of preparation, they are likely to respect her candor and hence find what she does say to be credible.

In any event, explanations or digressions that may be necessary to the advocate's position should follow rather than precede her response; else there is a good chance the response will not be given. Answer first, then, if necessary, explain.

Among the more difficult problems the advocate may have to face, if the bench is an active one, is how to deal with consecutive questions. The consecutive question problem has two variations. In the first, Judge Smith asks a question and either is interrupted by Judge Jones before she can complete it or is immediately followed by a question from Judge Jones before the advocate can respond to Judge Smith's inquiry. To whom should the advocate respond? If she responds to Judge Smith, Judge Jones may be offended; if to Judge Jones, Judge Smith may be offended. In either event, what of the substance of the question to which no immediate response has been made? The court may treat it with the same attitude as it does other questions to which an advocate does not respond.

Generally, the better practice is to respond first to the last judge to address the advocate. The judge who was interrupted or whose question was preempted will be likely to focus her resentment at least partly on her colleague rather than heaping it entirely on the advocate. Moreover, just as it is more natural in conversation to respond to the last speaker, so it is in the more formal setting of oral argument. If the second question and the response to it are relatively brief the advocate may wish to return to the preceding question immediately upon completing her answer. On the other hand, if her response is a lengthy one it may seem somewhat awkward to advert to the antecedent question immediately.

Sometimes the judge who first inquired will resolve the problem by repeating her initial inquiry when the advocate has finished responding to her colleague. Where that does not occur, however, the particular decision is a judgment call, dependent, in part at least, upon the advocate's sense of the particular bench. Experience will, of course, inform that judgment.

In any event, the advocate should do her best to see to it that before her argument is completed, the substance of the previously unanswered question is addressed. Moreover, if it is necessary to do this later in the course of the argument, the advocate should point out that she is now addressing those concerns. And she should do so not merely by calling attention to their substance but by recalling that it was Judge Smith who raised the issue. "As Judge Smith suggested earlier . . ." Such a formula accomplishes three things. First, it calls attention to the substance of what is to be said. Second, it reminds the court that the advocate has not left a question unanswered. Finally, and not unimportant, it tells Judge Smith that she has not been forgotten and that her question is sufficiently incisive and important to deserve a response.

The second variation of the consecutive question problem arises when the advocate is given the opportunity to respond to the first question but immediately upon concluding that response, or even before concluding it, is confronted with a new question from the same or a different judge, based not upon the advocate's principal argument but on her response to the first question. In this way, the advocate may be driven further and further afield from the argument she had planned and which she must make to prevail on the appeal. It is for this reason that the advocate's preparation must include several generations of questions from those arising immediately out of her principal argument. Even assuming, however, that the advocate is able to respond to these questions, how is she to get back on track, to return to her argument?

First, the techniques discussed in the preceding sections should be employed to minimize the problem. Specifically, there should be no pause between the advocate's response to a question and her return to the mainstream of her argument. As has been suggested, such moments of silence are invitations to the court to fill the void with another question. Because the last point made by the advocate will have been in response to a preceding question, the court is likely to take off from that point leading the advocate yet further from her planned presentation. Thus, one should always attempt to complete a response with some statement or proposition from which one can return to the main body of the argument. Nor is this as difficult as it sounds.

It is in the solution of this problem that one of the functions of a well thought out theme for one's case becomes clear. Because the argument's theme runs through virtually everything the advocate will say about the case, she can naturally return to it from any point in the argument. Moreover, she can advance to any point in the argument from her statement of the theme. It is like a great river from which one can emerge into smaller tributaries and to which one can return from those tributaries in order to move to any other tributary along the river. Of course, the advocate must avoid continually restating the theme in precisely the same form of words. But the basic proposition—the substance or sense of the theme—is perhaps the best vehicle with which to move easily within the argument from any point to any other point. Moreover, doing so will tend to reinforce that theme in the minds of the court and hence enable them to grasp and to retain the advocate's position with greater facility.

§ 8–12. Concluding

There are two contexts in which the problem of gracefully leaving the lectern may arise. First, the advocate may have said everything she wished and responded to any questions put by the court; second, the advocate's time may have expired before she was permitted to complete all (or even much) of her argument. These two contexts require somewhat different approaches.

In the first situation, perhaps the most important advice for the advocate who has completed her presentation with some of her time remaining concerns what not to do: She ought not continue. As we have suggested earlier, after making the points she sought to make, developing the position she had intended to develop, the best thing she can do is to conclude, thank the court, sit down and shut up. Yet all too often advocates—

especially neophytes or students involved in academic moot court exercises—believe it is poor form to fail to use all one's time. In this view, every moment that the advocate has to connect with the minds of the court should be used to the full.

If the advocate has completed all she had planned to present in its most developed form, however, there are only two things for which this remaining time can be used. First, the advocate may simply reiterate matter already covered. To do so, however, places the repeated material outside the previously determined structure of the case at the risk not only of weakening the reiterated point but the argument as a whole. There is also the danger of time expiring in the midst of the reiteration resulting in a weak and lingering conclusion. Finally, there is the risk that the court will perceive that the advocate is attempting merely to fill time. As a consequence, the court may conclude that the advocate was inadequately prepared or the court may simply cease paying attention to material they have already heard. And, of course, the end of one's presentation is the last time one wishes to lose the court's attention.

The second way the advocate may choose to fill her unexpired time is yet worse. She may simply begin to present material she has not prepared, to argue off the cuff. This is quite simply an invitation to disaster. Not only is one likely to be caught up in inconsistencies and contradictions and to demonstrate one's unpreparedness, but these weaknesses are quite likely to have a spill-over effect, turning what may have been a strong, cogent and persuasive argument into an unconvincing bit of fluff.

Thus, it is far, far better to finish strong, even when this requires the sacrifice of some of the time allotted to the advocate's presentation. Further, doing so suggests a certain confidence in one's position that may well affect the court's view of the argument advanced. Finally, such behavior indicates a sensitivity and consideration for the court that, while perhaps unacknowledged, is often appreciated.

The advocate in the position of having sufficient time to conclude as she wishes should take advantage of that luxury. An effective conclusion has a number of important attributes: It must be meticulously prepared; yet it should not sound as if it were being read or delivered from memory. Presented that way—prepackaged— even the strongest conclusion will be unconvincing. If the argument has been divided among two advocates, the first to conclude should sum up the points she has made and introduce her colleague, indicating as well the substance of her colleague's argument. The second advocate in a shared presentation must summarize the entire argument and request the specific action she wishes the court to take: affirm the decision below, reverse the decision below and remand with directions to perform some particular act, grant a new trial or issue some other appropriate mandate. It is perfectly permissible, indeed desirable, to request particular forms of relief in the alternative if that is otherwise appropriate. There is no inherent weakness in, for example, requesting a reversal of the decision below and a remand with directions to enter judgment for one's client or, in the alternative, requesting a new trial.

The summary itself should reflect the entire argument in microcosm. Thus, the structure of the summary should parallel the structure of the argument. Most important to the well prepared and well delivered summary is a reiteration of the advocate's theme of the case. That theme should, if possible, be the last substantive memory of the case left with the court. It should be emphasized once again, however, because the fault is such a common one, that though prepared with infinite care, the summary and conclusion of the argument should appear as naturally spontaneous in delivery as the body of the advocate's presentation. Eschew the canned conclusion!

The second and perhaps more common situation for which the advocate must be prepared is the expiration of time earlier than the advocate would have wished. Given careful preparation and attentiveness to the clock, the advocate ought to have presented at least her minimal argument by the time her time has expired.

It will sometimes happen that the advocate is made aware of the expiration of her time while a member of the bench is asking a question or in the midst of her answer to such a question. First, the advocate must advise the court that her time has expired. That statement should be followed by the tactical pause, during which, one hopes, the court will request the advocate to respond or to continue or even to take a moment to sum up or conclude. In the absence of such an invitation it may be permissible to request a moment to complete one's answer to a question. The propriety of such a request depends upon the custom in the particular court and ought to be investigated before the argument. Generally courts will permit a response to be concluded with greater forbearance than they will show for a request to conclude or sum up.

Sometimes, especially if the bench has been an active one, members of the court will continue to ask questions after expiration of the advocate's time. An advocate fortunate enough to be in this position should make the most of it; for it suggests that the court's interest has been aroused. And, of course, the advocate is then using the court's time, not her own. Very occasionally a hyperactive bench will take pity upon an advocate who has stood up to the apparently endless barrage of questions from the bench and may, without being asked, extend an additional short period of time for a brief summation of the advocate's position. This opportunity too should be exploited. It permits the advocate to conclude on the same terms as her colleague who was not required by the pressure of time to compress her summary.

Assuming that the court will permit a response that extends the established time limits, the advocate should so structure her response as to incorporate—at least in skeletal form—the prepared conclusion and reiteration of the theme as previously suggested. In the ideal world, the advocate completes a response by subtly segueing into her superbly crafted and delivered conclusion and summary, ending with a "thank you" to the court at precisely the moment she is informed of the expiration of time. Not surprisingly, such good fortune tends to be visited upon the skillful advocate that can so pace the last few minutes of her time as to foster this perfect conclusion.

Thus, like the preparation for the main body of the argument, preparation of the conclusion should proceed on more than one track. There should be a fully developed summary and conclusion as well as a skeletal version. Moreover, as is also true with respect to the main body of the argument, it is important to be able to get to one's conclusion from a number of different points in the argument; it may be difficult to predict what substantive issue one will be addressing as one's time begins to run out.

CHAPTER NINE

A FINAL NOTE: THE INTEGRITY OF ARGUMENT

It seems appropriate to end where we began—with the role and responsibilities of appellate advocacy, but also with its joys and satisfactions. It is through the appellate process that the lawyer has her greatest opportunity to make a mark on the development of the law. Admittedly, there can be much satisfaction for the office lawyer, counseling clients how to act, what to do to serve their interests and assisting them as well to discover what those interests may be; as planner, shaping the future to assure the execution of the wishes of her clients; as negotiator, peacemaker, helping resolve disputes to the satisfaction of those involved.

Similarly, there is much in which the trial lawyer can find pride and exhilaration: the shaping of a production consistent with doctrinal requirements at the same time that one is creating and maintaining dramatic interest and a coherent narrative, all the while attending the effects of each and every event occurring in the courtroom on judge and jury, with one eye always on the record. The excitement of combat, of pitting one's skills against the best one's adversary has to offer, and the immediacy of the result—the thrill of a favorable verdict, the disappointment of an unfavorable one—all this can make trial work a consuming legal adventure.

Yet the effect of any of these activities in a particular case is generally not of great significance beyond the parties immediately involved. That is certainly not to denigrate them; obviously these activities play a critical role in the just and efficient functioning of society. Nonetheless, a single appellate opinion from a court of last resort is likely to have far greater impact than any number of instances of the other sorts of lawyer's activities. The opportunity for the appellate advocate to contribute to this process, to assist in shaping the growth of the law is in part responsible for the attraction of this aspect of practice. The advocate's excitement in seeing the theory or ideas presented to the court incorporated into its opinion, to become a part of the *corpus juris* is not of the same kind as the trial lawyer's in hearing of a favorable verdict. But it is every bit as intense and deeply felt.

This opportunity imposes responsibility as well. All lawyers, of course, are obliged to protect and defend with vigor the rights and interests of those they represent. And this is equally true of the appellate advocate. Because of the lasting effect of appellate decisions, however, the appellate advocate also should view herself as obliged, consistent with her obligation to her client, to present her case with a somewhat larger view in mind. This is not—emphatically not—to say that the advocate should sacrifice the interests of her client to what she may perceive to be the better long term view. That is the job for which we have judges. It is merely to urge that even in the service of a client's position the coherent, rationally justified, principled argument should be selected in preference to the clever, short-term, good-for-this-case-only approach that one too often sees in our appellate court rooms.

Just as the responsibilities of the professional require loyalty, so too do they require competence. Competence requires mastery of one's craft. And mastery involves more than the achievement of the quick fix. It entails a concern with the integrity of one's product.

The sculptor at work on her statue, the poet on her verse, the painter on her canvas, all are engaged in translating some idea or vision into concrete terms. Their art is in some measure to be judged by the extent to which the translation is successful—the extent to which the product remains true to its central idea, true to itself. The absence of that idea or theme results in the haphazard or the arbitrary.

Argumentation too is an art. And, like other arts, is successful only when true to its animating force, when it possesses its own integrity. An argument's integrity requires that it follow its logos; that all its details be set by its animating theme. Arguments formed of bits and pieces, of the flotsam and jetsam of cases, quotations, unrelated facts, unenlightened passion fails as art, fails as advocacy, fails. To whatever extent an argument relies on mere cleverness, superficiality, glibness to overcome resistance, rather than tackling it on its own terms, the argument lacks integrity.

The development of an argument is a process of creation. As important as the responsibility to one's client and to the development of the law is the responsibility owed to the integrity of one's creative work. It is that, after all, that provides the deepest satisfaction to the artist—be she painter, sculptor or advocate. The integrity of the work is the measure of the artist; the integrity of the argument, the measure of the advocate.

Life's like that, too.

INDEX

References are to Pages

INDEX

References are to Pages

INDEX

References are to Pages

[*319*]

INDEX

INDEX

INDEX

[*324*]

INDEX

†